Advance Praise for
Anticipating Education: Concepts for Imagining Pedagogy with Psychoanalysis

"In *Anticipating Education*, Deborah Britzman draws on three decades' worth of profound reflection on education, seen through the prism of critical and psychoanalytic ideas. The result is a wonderful short book, in which she creates a tapestry of insightful and moving observations on how education can be revolutionised by thought that carries emotion and politics with it. Education emerges from this book as an essential catalyst for living a full life."

—Stephen Frosh, Professor in Psychosocial Studies
Birkbeck, University of London

"This book is a marvelous instance of the psychoanalytic truth which good educators must learn to work with, that we all inhabit a precarious life-world that is structured by anticipation and 'afterwardness'. Deborah Britzman gathers together earlier papers for us, supplementing them with typically thoughtful additional reflections on what is usually un-thought in pedagogical practice. Now we can rediscover how prescient all this is, and grasp the opportunity of benefitting from it before it is too late."

—Ian Parker, Secretary
Manchester Psychoanalytic Matrix

"In these exquisitely crafted essays, Deborah P. Britzman personifies her psychoanalytic state of mind, entering what she calls the crypt of curriculum, asking: "why curriculum at all?" This book is itself the resounding answer. Enlivening knowledge through her thinking, Deborah's insights invite us inside thought itself, where complicated conversation can commence. If you have—as I do—a shelf in your library devoted to Britzman, be sure to add this one. If space limits you to one Britzman book, make it this one."

—William F. Pinar, Tetsuo Aoki Professor in Curriculum Studies
University of British Columbia, Vancouver, Canada

"Dr. Britzman—leading international authority on psychoanalysis and education and practicing psychoanalyst—offers a collection of her work written with intellectual depth, immense virtuosity, and whole heart. Britzman's repertoire is wide-ranging as she instructs us why we must not forget there is no emotional situation-free zone for education. I can't think of any contemporary scholar and writer who has more poet in her soul; this volume will be one of the most treasured books in the field of psychoanalysis and education."

—Jenna Min Shim, Professor and Associate Dean
in College of Education, University of Wyoming

"Deborah Britzman has written so many beautiful books about pedagogy and psychoanalysis that you may be thinking 'why this one?' Hands down, this is Britzman's best book yet: lyrical, incisive, rigorous, true. The book is ultimately about love as the highest intellectual pursuit, and education as its vehicle. It is a tour de force. I could not put it down. In a world where students are more anxious than ever, and teachers stand at the threshold of burnout, you may be asking yourselves what we possibly can do now. Start here. Read this book."

—*Dawn Skorczewski, Research Professor Emerita*
Brandeis University

"This erudite and poetic book offers an invitation to return to the source of education, a place of vulnerability, anguish, wonderment and possibility. Beneath the "mind-numbing stultification" of bureaucratized schooling can be found teachers seeking to embrace childhood subjectivity and difference and release the imagination. This book is for such educators. In its expansiveness and vision, this book builds on the work of Paulo Freire and Maxine Greene to articulate a pedagogy of the imagination. Britzman illustrates the beautiful complementarity of psychoanalysis and critical educational theory in articulating a pedagogy of interiority, social justice, and creative possibility that so many educators hunger for."

—*Michael O'Loughlin, Adelphi University, New York*

ANTICIPATING EDUCATION

ANTICIPATING EDUCATION

Concepts for
Imagining Pedagogy
with Psychoanalysis

BY DEBORAH P. BRITZMAN

Gorham, Maine

Copyright © 2021 | Myers Education Press, LLC

Published by Myers Education Press, LLC
P.O. Box 424 Gorham, ME 04038

All rights reserved. No part of this book may be reprinted or reproduced in any form or by any electronic, mechanical, or other means, now known or hereafter invented, including photocopying, recording, and information storage and retrieval, without permission in writing from the publisher.

Myers Education Press is an academic publisher specializing in books, e-books, and digital content in the field of education. All of our books are subjected to a rigorous peer review process and produced in compliance with the standards of the Council on Library and Information Resources.

Library of Congress Cataloging-in-Publication Data available from Library of Congress.

13-digit ISBN 978-1-9755-0431-1 (paperback)
13-digit ISBN 978-1-9755-0430-4 (hardcover)
13-digit ISBN 978-1-9755-0432-8 (library networkable e-edition)
13-digit ISBN 978-1-9755-0433-5 (consumer e-edition)

Printed in the United States of America.

All first editions printed on acid-free paper that meets the American National Standards Institute Z39-48 standard.

Books published by Myers Education Press may be purchased at special quantity discount rates for groups, workshops, training organizations, and classroom usage. Please call our customer service department at 1-800-232-0223 for details.

Cover design by Teresa Lagrange

Cover art by Vahid Fazel, "The Traveler"

Visit us on the web at **www.myersedpress.com** to browse our complete list of titles.

Table of Contents

Acknowledgments — ix
Prelude: Late Education — xi

Part I: Phantasies Of Education

Chapter 1
A Note On Transference To Reading — 1

Chapter 2
On Not Being Able To Write — 5

Chapter 3
The Homoerotic Turn — 13

Chapter 4
Teacher Education In The Confusion Of Our Times — 21

Part II: Difficult Knowledge

Chapter 5
On Some Psychical Consequences of AIDS Education — 29

Chapter 6
The Death Of Curriculum? — 41

Chapter 7
The Fate Of Being A Stranger — 49

Part III: Transforming Subjects

Chapter 8
Public Education As States Of Mind — 59

Chapter 9
'Each To Each' And The Equality Of Vulnerability — 69

Chapter 10
Notes On The Poetics Of Supervision — 75

Chapter 11
Some Psychoanalytic Observations
On Ordinary, Quiet, And Painful Resistance — 89

Part IV: Psychoanalysis With Pedagogy

Chapter 12
'Even In Cambridge' — 101

Chapter 13
    What Is Emotional About Our Emotional Situation?   107
Chapter 14
    On Disquieting Imagination, Indeterminacy,
    Aesthetic Conflicts, And Grouch Days   113

About The Author   121
Index of Selected Concepts For Imagining Pedagogy With Psychoanalysis   123

Acknowledgments

Parts of this book originally appeared in the edited volumes of others and as articles in journals. Other chapters were given as lectures and as conference papers. I thank the following for permission to reprint previous work:

I acknowledge Taylor & Francis Ltd, for their permission to reprint Chapters 3, 4, 5, 10, and 11 (Taylor & Francis Ltd, http://www.tandfonline.com). I thank Peter Lang Press for permission to reprint Chapter 6.

Chapter 1: (2020). Appeared as "A Note on Free Association as Transference to Reading "in *The SAGE Handbook of Critical Pedagogy Vol.1*, chapter 4, edited by Shirley Steinberg and Barry Down, 17-19. Thousand Oaks, CA: Sage Publications.

Chapter 3: (2017). "The Homoerotic Turn and Currere." Originally published in *The Reconceptualization of Curriculum Studies: A Festschrift in Honor of William F. Pinar*, edited by M. Doll, 27-34. New York: Routledge Press.

Chapter 4: (2000). "Teacher Education and the Confusion of Our Time." *Journal of Teacher Education* 51 (3): 200–5.

Chapter 5: (1998). "On Some Psychical Consequences of AIDS Education." Originally published in *Queer Theory and Education*, edited by W. Pinar, 321–36. Mahwah, NJ: Lawrence Erlbaum Publishers.

Chapter 6: (2002). "The Death of Curriculum?" Originally published in *Curriculum Visions*, edited by W. Doll and N. Gough, 92–101. New York: Peter Lang.

Chapter 7: (2003). Parts of chapter 7 were originally published as "That Uncertain Fate." *International Journal of Educational Leadership: Theory and Practice* 6 (1): 4–9.

Chapter 9: A section of "Each to Each" on "Sammy the scribe" is an earlier version of a longer discussion found in Britzman (2015), *A Psychoanalysis in the Classroom*. Albany: State University of New York Press.

Chapter 10: (2009). "The Poetics of Supervision: A Psychoanalytic Thought Experiment for Teacher Education." *Changing English* 16 (4): 385–96.

Chapter 11: (2010). "Some Psychoanalytic Observations on Quiet, Ordinary and Painful Resistance." *International Journal of Leadership in Education* 13 (3): 239–48. doi:10.1080/13603124.2010.496874

Prelude: Late Education

> *What does it mean to return to sources?... The source of inspiration is nothing other than the object of the search.*
> —JEAN LAPLANCHE, "EXIGENCY AND GOING AWAY"

IF ONE COULD return to the sources of education, to where we all began, where would one be and with whom? What causes could be remembered? Who would we be thinking of? Such questions imagine education as a state of mind and the object of our search. The papers arranged in this volume, which span from around 1993 through to 2020, reside in this temporality of anticipating education. Some have been previously published while others were given as talks. Looking back, I can remember each of their writing occasions and still marvel over what their demands felt like. But their sources have a longer gestation, already inscribed well before memories of their writing. The urgencies that belong to anticipation are beholden to the rough drafts of infancy, extended by childhood inexperience of trying to know without knowing why, and met again with uncanny feelings left over from having spent much of my life waiting, wanting, wishing, and anticipating education. Memories of education return as inner life. They are affected and effectuate flutters of incompleteness, uncertainty, anxieties, and even the defense of confusion. So, I express all this as emotional situations and as relations made from trying to represent untold problems of and obstacles within teaching and learning.

I am interested in exploring some psychical consequences of education through the fate of feelings education leaves in its wake and by questioning what qualities of education can be projected forward. I can summarize my key preoccupations this way: Education as both a field of thought and the grounds for its own social practices is subject to what history cannot complete and society neither absorbs nor acknowledges. By definition, education inherits our incompleteness as it is always a question of how we learn to live. As a constellation of upbringing, institutions, cultural imperatives, idealizations, arguments, professional training, and phantasies of learning, experience in education becomes affected by what is most unresolved within our knowledge of self in the world with others. Within these complexities of uneven development, we recreate education as our emotional situation. We may be asked to let go of the meanings we felt were already settled. We may find that the curriculum contains deceptive views. We may realize that there is no semblance between what is on offer and our deepest investments for wanting to become a self. And we may wish to unsettle the unsatisfying and stultifying meanings provided. For reasons of complexity, we in education—from nursery through to university life—have the ongoing work of creating an ethical turn that can accommodate not understanding, the limits of knowledge, and feelings of uncertainty. We have the ongoing work of noticing and transforming what prohibits an open mind.

With four major frames of this volume—phantasies of education, difficult knowledge, transforming subjects, and psychoanalysis with pedagogy—I take a second look at the emotional situations of teaching and learning. To reside within the movements between psychical reality and external reality, I treat the time of education as oscillating between 'there and then' and 'here and now.' The structures, functions, interactions, transferences, identifications, and concepts that render education intelligible or sadly out of date, after all, are affected by the lives we each live and by what came before, the feel of it now, and the wait for a future one can neither know nor predict. We can ask how the inside experience of education proceeds through transitional scenes of inheriting a past one could not make while experiencing the demands of the present one has never expected. And I see these processes as opening onto the dynamics of affecting concerns underway by asking what thinking life is like because we are subjects in and of education. All told, by highlighting psychoanalytic methods of interpretation and by bringing psychoanalytic concepts to imagine the inner world of pedagogy, learning and teaching can now be regarded as states of mind. Dear readers, don't be alarmed! Together we can imagine states of mind as constitutionally relational and made with the urgencies of anxiety and the potentials of reparative capacities that can link promises of care and toleration to the creation of new social bonds. The need is for the valence of thinking, free association, and transference to narrative freedom. The desire is for creating a personal education in the presence of others, near and far and here and gone. The challenge is to care for the vulnerabilities of bodies and minds as sources of inspiration.

Mistaken Education

I entered the teaching profession by accident, even as my late psychoanalytic training forced me to consider the oddities of experience as unconsciously motivated. Like so many others about to graduate from high school without really knowing much about the kind of education I was in for or even wanted, I applied to the university. Because I liked the topic, I thought I had signed up for the history department. Not until I received the university's letter of acceptance that welcomed me to the School of Education did I learn I had checked the wrong box. At the time, I worried that if I were to reapply to the university, I would not be accepted. I felt I had missed my only chance.

I was one of those students who found high school painful and lonely. Yes, there were school librarians and English teachers who believed the searching mind was permitted to matter. And it seemed that the complexity of novels given to me by those teachers and librarians, along with how they conveyed their own love of literature, was more needed than the nagging feeling that my intellectual and emotional interests were worthless in the daily regime of compliance to high school life. I attended a rural high school in a small racially and ethnically segregated town. The high school adhered to harsh disciplinary procedures: corporal punishment, suspensions, military recruitment days, Christian prayers that began the morning loudspeaker announcements, and strict dress codes for girls and boys. Each and every strategy of control felt persecutory. Of about 1,500 adolescents in the high school, three of us were Jewish and one of them was my brother. There I learned the fate of being a stranger.

I hoped the university would not be conservative, narrow-minded, or authoritarian. I already knew contentious education due to university student protest movements for civil rights and against the United States' involvement in the Vietnam War. During my high school years, males 18 years old were forced into a draft lottery for military conscription. Those against the war either fled from the United States to Canada, went to jail, signed into the field of education at the university for a teaching deferral, or figured out a medical exemption. During an anti-war student protest in the spring of 1970 at Kent State University in Ohio, the state governor ordered the national guard to clear protesters from campus. The National Guard shot and killed four university students. There were many such scenes of violence across university campuses. I lived about a half-hour away from Kent State University and knew the deep conservatism of southern Ohio. My high school did not have sympathy for the student demonstrators. In their calls for law and order, many teachers and parents felt the students deserved to be killed. The murder of university students and the violence of authoritarian education radicalized a new generation of high school and university students who articulated the politics of education, the practices of leaving classrooms for 'teach-ins,' and the writing of pamphlets that helped organize more student demonstrations and fought for education to change. In that spring of 1970, many universities across the United States closed early due to student protests and political unrest.

When I received my letter of university admission to the School of Education, my worst nightmare felt true. In 1970, the School of Education resembled a Normal School, the earliest version of teacher education dedicated to training elementary school teachers. Requirements included piano lessons, instructions in proper handwriting, speech therapy for any student who spoke English with a strong accent, and directives on gendered dressing. Professionalism was defined by the belief in the certainty of rules. I entered this world with sinking feelings that I had never left the terrors of high school. By Fall midterm, without finishing my first introduction to education course, I was given a failing grade, judged unfit to teach. I was placed into another course section and there received a high mark. However, the faculty blended the first course grade with the second, and I received another failure. It took a number of hearings and petitions to remove the failing grade from my transcript. Two years later, with the help of Dr. Warren Bennis, then president of the University of Cincinnati, I transferred to the School of Education at the University of Massachusetts in Amherst. The year was 1972. There I experienced the frisson of public alternative education, the protests and practices of de-schooling and decolonizing education, the abolishment of grades, and the strategies and modes of interaction made from antiracist and antisexist education and from gay and lesbian liberation. With these politics of education, I celebrated radical teachers. I graduated at the age of 21 and moved to Hartford, Connecticut, to work as an English teacher in a public alternative high school. The school was located in a set of trailers sitting in a parking lot of a large high school. We specialized in not fitting in, and as teachers, used to joke that the alternative school was the last gas station before the desert.

Looking back almost 50 years later, I had to experience many more teaching and learning encounters and a move from the United States to Canada to realize that education—whether occurring in nursery and compulsory school or whether in university and professional programs—is also a state of mind. As an evolving emotional situation, education becomes subject to the procedures of psychical life, and with our conflicts with external reality, when we teach and learn, we, too, are subject to sensate feelings of uncertainty, anxiety, and wishes for change.

Matters of Psychoanalysis With Pedagogy

I have been a teacher and professor longer than I have been a psychoanalyst. While I did not check the wrong box, I still managed to enter another impossible profession based in trying to get to know the movements between subjectivity and intersubjectivity and between internal objects and relations with external others.

In learning that third profession of psychoanalysis, thoughts about the meanings of my previous education took on new editions of these old conflicts. I became a volunteer for the unconscious and for the emotional nature of biphasic learning from the latency and awakening of education, mine and others. Just as with education, the clinic of psychoanalysis may be thought of as a frame for holding practice, as a set of theories on the nature and affectivity of mental life, as investigating and appreciating the primacy of the other, and as techniques and terms of engagement, all of which are subject to further interpretative work. John Forrester (2017) described these interpersonal events as "thinking in cases" that involve the pleasures and dangers of trying to understand the mind of the other with one's own mind. But it does take the other to create a mind that can then imagine the other. While it may seem strange to think of education as a clinic, this need not be the case. Following, Gilles Deleuze's (1997) literary treatment of the clinical and the critical, I too propose to orient theories of learning to a pedagogical field of symptoms, treatment, conditions, experiences, causes, desires, and therapeutic action. I add to the clinic of education Julia Kristeva's (1989) view of psychoanalysis as "counter-depressant" (1) and, with Kristeva, can think of education as a treatment of thought, desire, and language. As odd as this may sound, the educator can work against inhibition and the repression of subjectivity.

Both psychoanalysis and education depend on the intersubjective relations and phantasies of its practitioners, researchers, students, and patients. Both fields lean on and may bother anyone's subjective sensitivities. But while they also attempt to address anxiety for various publics, they may each be blamed for causing anxiety. As I work from within both fields, I have noticed important differences between them while handling difficulties, uncertainties, and obstacles to life's challenges.

Psychoanalytic views of the human condition propose at least five major frames that allow me to understand the conflicts within and breakdowns in pedagogical relations. First, psychoanalysis privileges the poetics, dynamics, and functions of psychical reality as expressed through the drives, phantasy, and the transference. While the outside world matters for us all, psychoanalysis is interested in the subject's problem of not being able to change while still waiting, wanting and needing change. It is interested in asking, what holds me back? Second, psychoanalysis calls upon estranged temporality such as what is experienced in dreams and felt within the transference exchange of authority and love. The unconscious is welcomed. Sleep becomes our best model for experiencing timelessness and our capacity to create dreams. Third, analysts learn to listen to what they do not know and do so through their affective responses, thought about as countertransference. The analyst is affected by the other and by the otherness of each of their respective histories. Behind the scenes the analyst's task is to understand her own participation and personal motivation in the creation of relationships. Fourth, there is a focus on the incidental, the accident, the misheard, and what is brushed aside as unmeant or meaningless. There is an interest in the fictions of intersubjective life. The expansive work seeks to draw significance from the experience of broken links by freely associating with unmeant phenomena, dreams, parapraxis, jokes, fantasies, obstacles, and even daydreams. And fifth, because the psychoanalytic field is concerned with its own therapeutic action and what it can mean to be instructed by one's work, analysts must continue to argue over the meanings of resistance, the problems of giving and receiving interpretation, and how the talking and listening cure affects the nature of anyone's capacity to change minds. Change depends on interpreting the shifting sands of language and affect and in doing that, finding anew the value of meanings tucked away and often alluding to events so far away that they are never thought of as affecting the currency of our attitudes, concepts, and desires. The analyst learns to wait for the other and for history to arrive.

It is with our fifth difference for how and why changing minds occur that psychoanalysis opens onto the complications, uncertainties, anxieties, and conflicts within learning relations. Psychoanalysis supposes a universal, extra-historical, original psychical apparatus as source, motive, mythology, and reason that functions as the soft ground for the pathos of the human condition. Except for the primacy of the other, there is no single source of inspiration that can give us a reason for why we have a mind at all or why the mind can go missing. Given this constitutional uncertainty, thought about as overdetermination, psychical life is mainly handled as an intersubjective impression and, as a consequence of birth, it is psychical life that affects our capacity for anticipation, frustration, love, hate, and our susceptibility to unknown influences. But unconscious forces within psychical time resist ego insight. This is an unusual claim for a theory of learning that attempts to contain the anxiety, frustration, and pain of incompleteness fashioned from the interactions of three dimensions of reality: material reality, historical events, and psychical reality. I suggest that these indeterminant sources and pulls of competing realities decenter the work of learning and, more often than we know, leave us anticipating or dreading what can and cannot touch the ways we think and feel.

Ever since Freud termed psychoanalysis as an 'after education,' psychoanalysis can be described in so many ways. Jonathan Lear's (2000) introduction to the writing of Hans Loewald suggested that since psychoanalysis is committed to a truth it cannot know in advance, the work qualifies as a "science of subjectivity" (xx). Jose Infante's (1995) discussion on Freud's views of phantasy, creative writing, and daydreams proposes psychoanalysis as "therapy of fate" (61) in that one reconceives on purpose what chance has created. One looks back to put the past into its place so there can be a destiny yet to be written. Jean Laplanche (1999) proposes psychoanalysis as a "radical decentering" of the ego with the work of deconstruction (60). And for Forrester (2017), psychoanalysis invites "new forms of accounting for the self" (14). Its interpretive style draws on the procedures of the dream work: refusal of negation, reversal into its opposite, condensation, substitution, consideration of representation, and the toleration of contradictions.

Four Frames

The experience of anticipation hardly needs explanation, for it is a sensate bodily set of events that involves our excitement, thoughts, projections, and phantasies of what can or may not happen. It is a conditional world of 'what if' that can go no further and, as heralds of anxiety, anticipation holds a special sounding that announces what has already happened, namely, numerous separations and losses of love. There are expectations, projections into time, worries that hopes will be dashed, feelings of being too late, and, perhaps, there are wishes for pleasant surprises. Anticipation is an emotional situation and an object relation. As a state of mind, it can refer to heightened awareness or high alert. Anticipating education has this flavor: we can expect something good or bad and worry that the education we find may not be the one we want. Another meaning involves us in experiences on hold, that is, as waiting rooms for something to happen. Here we are involved in a strange situation that calls upon our projections, defenses, phantasies, and desires. Illusions and disillusions seem to qualify the time of anticipation.

Each of the four frames in this volume emerges from scenes of anticipating education. Phantasies of education compose the first frame and provide orientations to memories of reading and writing, to inhibitions and blocks in creativity, to homosocial experiences and longings for a gay education, and for living within confusions of our time. The concept of phantasies is drawn from psychoanalytic vocabulary and is beholden to the object relations theories of Melanie Klein, who considered the mind as our fundamental phantasy. While Klein plays a strong role in many of my discussions, this first frame introduces her views of phantasies as a function of psychical and social life, as states of mind, as emotional investment, and as the mechanisms made to express, split, deny, project, and internalize anxieties, dreams, wishes, and defenses. Phantasies can be thought of as the fractious half time summary of anticipations of disaster and lost satisfaction. They are due to the psychological fact that we feel before we know while seemingly certain that we know before we can understand. But this means that learning involves a particular deferral and our phantasy life. By design, phantasies are relational, fantastical, defensive, tender, hostile, and unconscious. They serve as conductors for the attractions of ideology, beliefs, modes of attachment and dissociation, and for styles of loving and hating. Phantasies thus give conviction or reality to felt sensations of emotional situations, screen memories, sexual feelings, and experiences of inhibition and creativity. Such are the complications for the case of writing inhibitions, a particular and painful symptom of education. Major conflicts of self and other revolve around how these phantasies are to be interpreted, just at the point when one tries to symbolize experiences that have been forgotten, disclaimed or misunderstood. The first frame lays the groundwork for an object relations approach to teaching and learning.

The second frame is made from difficult knowledge, a phrasing I first used to describe trauma as a conceptual and ethical problem for pedagogy. It signals felt wordlessness, shock, and even sorrow as qualities of learning made from the history of the reception of human-induced catastrophe and the confrontation of denial in pedagogical time. Difficult knowledge signifies sadness, remorse, pining, memory, and the urge to repair. The idea of difficult knowledge leans on the force felt from inheriting the presence of history yet to be thought and emotionally acknowledged. Given that education inherits what the social cannot resolve and that courses of study involve the incompleteness of understanding history, I developed the conceptual frame of difficult knowledge around 1992 as a means to study breakdowns and restorations of meaning in university curriculum. The ethical difficulty involves linking arguments over the valence of social change and human rights to an interest in the study of obstacles to opening minds (Britzman 1998).

In considering the study of difficult knowledge, my first articulation involved how to have education in a pandemic. The pandemic belonged to the social disavowal of HIV/AIDS. Another way of putting this is how to have education in situations of profoundly painful inequality and identity disparagement. I began with questions. What states of mind are needed to study and care for the experience, symbolization, and development of HIV/AIDS? What states of mind can create courage of thought to account for the cultural illness of the social body? How can we study social denial with creative resistance? Is there a queer pedagogy that can help us? (Britzman 1995). By the early 1990s, most students born after 1980 did not know a world without HIV/AIDS and did not know that the subject of AIDS contained a history of reception in activism, cultural expressions of gay and lesbian life, and a long history of opening the closet. I learned that undergraduate and graduate students hardly had the invitation to study the cultural shifts, protests against hatred and prejudice, and linguistic transformations created by

AIDS activists, literary and visual artists, educators, and cultural theorists. Many did not know the history of gay and lesbian pride and the ways activism linked sexuality and the freedom to love with the desire for social change. Many of the students and professors I encountered had never read a gay or lesbian novel or, if they had, did not know who they were reading. Some students were very far away from the pathos of loss and the structure of feeling created by this early pandemic and could not answer the question, Why care? For those studying to become teachers, when asked to think about AIDS in education, they could only imagine unsafe blood transfusions and infected children. They could not imagine that the AIDS pandemic mainly affected adult teachers. I came to understand that one of the large obstacles to thinking the fate of education was involved in how we can convey a picture of education as more than what happens to children and as something affecting adults in schools and universities. And the idea of a language of AIDS as more than the technical affair of safer sex was hardly thinkable. While much has changed and while HIV is now considered as treatable illness, pandemics have not ended. As new pandemics emerge, studies of responses to HIV/AIDS can, I think, continue to serve as an exemplary case for designing capacious theories and expressions of cultural change as our education. In this second frame, other forms of difficult knowledge emerge with studies on the fate of being a stranger expressed in literature and psychoanalysis. Imagining the death of the curriculum may also be a mode of difficult knowledge.

Transforming subjects, our third frame, explores relations of learning as a change of mind as opposed to an accrual of knowledge. Chapters in this frame focus on needed cultural shifts and revolts mainly due to the creativity of new generations sick and tired of compliance in education and mind-numbing stultification. It is here I develop the idea of education as a state of mind that can experience affecting concerns underway. Such an approach takes the side of vulnerability and dependency as our original source for learning and teaching and proposes the case for rethinking compliance and resistance to change in our professional practices. This frame also suggests what the field of education can learn from the psychoanalytic studio of supervision.

Psychoanalysis with pedagogy composes the fourth frame with the focus on anticipating the influence of others on the ways we work and think. There is also the problem of remembering what influence feels like. Topics in this fourth frame include: the lost early history of Freud in the university; relational difficulties in writing biographies with the emotional quest for identification with one's subject; and, a reflection on the influences of friendship, growing old, loss, and thinking from the pain of incompleteness.

Anticipating education has many dimensions: turn one way to find an adult looking back to her first-grade reading group and remembering what it once felt like to need to steal a book. With another turn catch a glimpse of a lonely child standing in line and waiting to move forward. Another turn permits memories to fade away, bleed into new scenes, and then dissolve into forgetting. Any return to what is no longer risks imagination for the certainties of experience. Imagination may be our best means for treating our phantasies of education that often defend against new and uncertain encounters.

The risk for imagination mirrors the risks of learning and teaching. We must involve ourselves in the sequelae of uncertainty, belatedness, and deferral of meanings and use these frayed experiences as the sources for our search for inspiration. If we already know that slugging education makes us nervous, we can also then ask why. We can ask, What has happened to us? What have we made happen for others? How odd is it to claim that a most difficult challenge humans give to one another belongs to learning to find love and risks changing closed minds into opening ones? What sort of anticipation comes with these freedoms?

Bibliography

Britzman, Deborah P. 1998. *Lost Subjects, Contested Knowledge: Toward a Psychoanalytic History of Learning*. Albany: State University of New York Press.

———. 1995. "Is There a Queer Pedagogy? Or, Stop Reading Straight." *Educational Theory* 45 (2): 151-166.

Deleuze, Gilles. 1997. *Essays Critical and Clinical*. Minneapolis: University of Minnesota Press.

Forrester, John. 2017. *Thinking in Cases*. Cambridge, UK: Polity Press.

Infante, Jose A. 1995. "Some Reflections on Phantasy and Creativity." In *On Freud's 'Creative Writers and Day-Dreaming,'* edited by Ethel Spector, Peter Fonagy, and Servulo Augusto Figueira, 53–64. New Haven, CT: Yale University.

Kristeva, Julia. 1989. *Black Sun: Depression and Melancholia*. Translated by Leon Roudiez. New York: Columbia University Press.

Laplanche, Jean. 1999. *Essays on Otherness*. Edited by John Fletcher. London: Routledge Press.

———. 2006. "Exigency and Going Astray." *Psychoanalysis, Culture & Society* 11 (2): 185–89.

Lear, Johnathan. 2000. "Introduction." In *The Essential Loewald: Collected Papers and Monographs*, by Hans W. Loewald, xix–xl. Hagerstown, MD: University Publishing Group.

CHAPTER 1

A Note On Transference To Reading

WOULD IT BE so far afield to relate Paulo Freire's (1983) 'The Importance of the Act of Reading' and his return to 'the most remote experiences of childhood' (5) with that of a psychoanalyst who listens in on her own case history? And, given that Freire mainly wished to comment on the significance of reading to his own life and to the creation of his pedagogical acts, might I, too, take a chance and freely associate to signs along the way and ask the affecting question, 'Why is there a desire to read?' Might I, too, search for lost traces of my long-ago childhood and link this prehistoric past to the currency of my commitments to protecting and caring for the life of the mind? Might I, too, narrate the transference, both positive and negative, both with love and hate, to reflect on what has become of my reading education? And, if I can do that, would I then open a new reading, a new world, and a new approach to old and seemingly intractable conflicts? Might I, too, find that what reading teaches is that nothing is what it seems to be, that reality, too, must pass through my subjective world and that within the act of interpreting there is an allowance for our earliest mental paradox, namely, that we are always reading for what cannot be seen but can still be imagined?

One day, over 60 years ago, when I was once six years old and there in my first-grade class, the teacher ordered me into the 'bad' readers group. I then stumbled upon the strange fact that I was going to be known as a slow reader. My first grade had four reading groups: the good, the almost good, the not-so-good, and the truly terribly bad. All children knew that the pretense of the names of the groups—let's call them the butterflies, the bees, the frogs, and the fishes—were mere cover stories for whether or not one was either good or bad. There was no such thing as the 'good enough' reader. The bad (dumb) group was given a very stupid thin book of gigantic type. Each page held a large picture and a few repetitive words: 'See Skip jump.' 'Jump Skip jump.' 'Jump, Jump, Jump.' *Ad nauseam*. The good (smart) group had a beautiful thick book filled with stories of adventures. I felt humiliated, jealous, and desperate. I had no idea how I could leave the dumb group. Indeed, besides the fact that my parents were getting a terrible divorce and besides the fact that I had stopped talking, I had no idea why I was there. One day, when the teacher was not looking, I went to the bookshelf and stole the smart book. I placed that book under my coat and left school with the stolen smart book. I was very worried my mother would ask how I came to possess the book. So, I hid it under my bed and only took it out to read when I was sure I would not be disturbed or caught. But I worried I would be accused of stealing the book. And I fantasied that my teacher would march to my house, demand that I confess, and take the book away. Near the end of that first year, still worried that I could not explain why I had the book at all, I threw the book out of my bedroom window. It landed on the flat part of the roof just below my window. For the next few years, I watched the weather destroy the book until there was hardly a sign of my crime. I hoped no one would learn that I had stolen and then destroyed a schoolbook. Reading was not only dangerous. Reading was my most complex emotional situation and my most obsessive fantasy.

In the naïveté of a young child—where reason and unreason and desire and anxiety feel one and the same—I could not imagine telling the teacher I wanted to read. I symbolically equated my desire to read with a crime and with feelings of guilt. Somehow, I was really able to steal words and the words knew that. Of course, childhood is that privileged time when there is no difference between the animate and the inanimate and feelings were everywhere and attributed to anything. And in childhood, our transference to objects felt as powerful as did the transference of love, hate, and authority onto actual people. Yet I have to wonder today, what could it mean that I would learn the desire to read by stealing a book? Like Freire (1983), who needed to assure his audience that the act of reading was and remains an emotional experience even as these affecting ties design intellect, I, too, must proclaim that in reading I was not 'a rationalist in boy's clothing' (6). I was, however, a fabulist with the capacity for imagining the worst and by hiding in sheep's clothing, or so I thought, had the illusion that I could escape my dumb fate and freely associate to my desire as a reader. I came to learn that just as with people, there would be transference to books loved and hated, understood and misunderstood, given and stolen. Only later did I learn why.

Sigmund Freud ([1899] 1968) has made the argument that our earliest memories involve two nearly opposing experiences—the actual and the imagined. Both are affected by leftover time, by the ripples of impressions. Both are incomplete and have to be that due to childhood itself. He described this complex as 'screen memories,' fragments of one event displaced from the original scene and projected onto another later event. It was Freud's answer to the common questions of why people tend to remember irrelevant or indifferent things, why people idealize a past never experienced, why we need a cover story, and why memory and forgetting are two sides of the same coin. The feeling of an event persists but the historical event is subject to the ravages of time, fractured and displaced, just like the decaying book thrown onto the roof of my childhood home. Memory is just that construction. Freud also compared approaching psychical life, or taking a case history, to an archeological dig. The bits of pottery and material signs of everyday ancient life are in fragments and scattered across a wide swath of land due to the weight of the earth, the work of worms, and nature's capacity for burial. The archeologist cannot be sure if the fragment found remained in its original place or, whether the bit of pottery had shifted to another location. But the metaphor of archeology could not quite address the liveliness of these fragments in mind. While modern scientific instruments might aid in clarifying the time, date, and place of an object, the same cannot be said of the objects of human feelings and the traces of those feelings that return at a moment's notice, say, when staring out of one's window and hallucinating a decaying book, still there on the roof. Our modern measurements cannot grasp what the desire to read feels like.

I would have to say that reading is not only an interpretive act. It is also one of imagination and how the mind functions that involves attention, reception, hallucination, bodily action, refinding, and memory. Reading forms associative pathways between the inner and outer world. There is something before interpretation and it has to do with transference, our susceptibility to our projections of life's impressions, to the act of becoming absorbed and lost in the other's words, and to the desire to escape into reading. Then memories of reading are like taking account of one's case history. Details slowly become a story of revision. Reading is an act of projective identification and imagination for, after all, words must signify what is no longer there. In reading we are able to associate with absence, a general principle for the capacity for symbolization. Something stands in for something else but cannot be the original thing. This little lesson, that the book can stand in for a crime, for a secret, for a six-year-old's emotional situation also brings a second chance to make a better world with a self that is less naïve, more assertive, and freer to associate disparate and fractured torso memories into a new narrative. And all these dynamic associations lend the mind its freedom and openness to things unseen so as to risk what happens to the self when one reads the dreams of transference to words and world.

Bibliography

Freire, Paulo. 1983. "The Importance of the Act of Reading." *Journal of Education* 165 (1): 5–11.

Freud, Sigmund. (1899) 1968. "Screen Memories." In *The Standard Edition of the Complete Psychological Works of Sigmund Freud, Volume III (1893–1899): Early Psycho-Analytic Publications*, edited and translated by James Strachey, in collaboration with Anna Freud, 303–22. London: Hogarth Press.

CHAPTER 2

On Not Being Able To Write

To begin...

Consider matters of creativity and inhibition as two sides of the same coin and as what is tossed away in education. The metaphor gambles with what we believe is our due and not only because we have all grown up in school and leave its doors with strong ideas—good and bad, better or worse—as to what learning should be like and how it should feel. The problem does come down to what can be said of education since the idea of education signifies a process, a function, the results of the process, and second thoughts as to its value and what is missing. So, too with the question of inhibition and creativity. These two are processes, functions of the mind, and results of their processes. They come with second thoughts as to their reasons, values, and losses.

My interest in both inhibition and creativity emerges from my work as a university professor, where students and faculty are urged to write, and indeed, many do want to write but, somehow, have lost their way. My work as a psychoanalyst provides another view. I see individuals who feel stuck, worry about failure or becoming disengaged, worry they are not creative, and worry they cannot try something unexpected in their daily life. For some, time has stopped. They turn the clock back when they ask, What if the same thing happens again? Others say they lose interest too quickly or feel it is just too late to try something new. They begin a project with enthusiasm and then just as suddenly stop. I see the same situation with those just beginning therapy. There is great hope for meaningful change but little patience for getting to know the self. So how does one study discontentment, disappointment, and loss of love? What do these feelings have to do with creativity and anticipating education?

Much of my thinking that proposes or anticipates negation is beholden to Marion Milner's (1990) self-study of her own inhibitions, *On Not Being Able to Paint*. Milner had the significant idea that it was important to study her failures and places of discontentment. Her interest was with trying to express unconscious emotional attitudes toward the nature of the creative process and in their convictions that reverse their course and provoke the failures to create.

Milner learned to find emotional attitudes woven in any scene, fleeting worry, or phantasy that make up one's state of mind. She analyzed creativity and inhibitions as emotional situations and commentary on the feel of psychical reality. So it seems right to engage Milner's approach to creativity and question what is occurring when, in education, we hear the common anxiety of not being able to write or not being able or allowed to be creative. And it seems right to study inhibitions and creativity as a means of getting to know the fluid boundaries of inner and outer reality. What then are the dangers and risks of imagination?

For Milner (1990), self-study is the grounds for symbolizing what imagination risks and she insists that imagination risks the destruction of meaning. She named this plunge into uncharted thoughts "the dangers inherent in imagination" (14) and included movements between the personal and the aesthetic, conflicts between subjective impressions and objective worlds, and procedures of creativity and anxiety. Milner wrote from the obscurities of her life: the things unclear or dissatisfying, the mishaps and misshapen experience, and the writer's incomplete, failed, or baffling encounters. As Milner admits, the desire for mastery may also be felt whenever one tries to write something new, and whenever one has to begin with the blank page. Mastery already indicates anxiety over the unknown and paradoxically, the wish for perfection may be a clue for an incapacity to be affected by symbolization.

Only gradually did Milner (1990) understand that to paint, the painter must surrender to both a wandering, aimless mind and be contained by what she called "facts of art" (127) that involve the acceptance of beginning with a blank canvas or frame, an interest in one's own limits, and attention to the critical play that structures and divides objectivity and subjectivity, and reality and phantasy. She used the idea of frame as both space and time: as a border, or canvas that contains the edges of a painting and as time, there are also rules of comportment. In Milner's words, "[t]hus when there is a frame it surely serves to indicate that what's inside the frame has to be interpreted in a different way from what's outside it" (157).

Misgiving And Giving

I have come to understand Milner's (1990) *On Not Being Able to Paint* as a method for the study of uncertainty in creative expression. Over the years, I have returned to her book. My recent reading was inspired by a discussion I had with a painter who, like Milner, felt dissatisfied with her painting but could not say why. This painter knew I thought of myself as a writer and in the painter's mind, that meant that I could not understand what it feels like to paint and not paint. This painter felt that painting was so different from writing that not only were the activities incomparable in physicality, interest, mood, grip, and medium. The writer and the painter could not meet. I still wonder what it is to understand another's creative processions. Would that be empathy, as if I could put myself in the painter's shoes? Or would it be more like witnessing the intricacies of the painter's entanglements and with that, wondering about my own?

As I read Milner with the other in mind, I wondered then what the writer could learn from the painter and, even more specifically, what the writer can learn from the agitations of the painter's body in the act of painting.

Milner wanted to understand the beginning of object relations as psychic creativity. She described these concepts as if they mirrored the activities that go into painting: contact with a pre-logical area of the mind characterized by fusion, illusions, reverie, concentration, absentmindedness, and a temporary loss of self that surrenders to ecstasy.

Part of Milner's book wrestled with her inhibitions and essentially a fear of creativity. No one can tell you how to have an inhibition, but once it seems to creep into one's mind, how difficult it is to know what is really being avoided.

Milner, who also wrote under the name 'Joanne Fields,' had a few careers: first, a teacher of reading in early childhood and then as an industrial psychologist for her first study of unhappiness in work. She returned to education, serving as researcher/interviewer for a five-year study of underachieving girls that resulted in a 1938 book, *The Human Problem of Schools*, edited by Susan Isaacs (Letley 2014). That study and the reports that followed discussed basic principles of children's learning, and this left her depressed. Schools, Milner found, are unhappy places (Farley 2015). In an overview of her career, Milner (1996) portrayed her work along with her sense of self as trying to understand the underlying yearnings of human behavior through picturing the forces of the unconscious life and imagination. Her introduction to *On Not Being Able to Paint*, and what I see as the true part, acknowledged her questions and "private misgivings" (xviii). "It was only gradually," Milner wrote in her preface, "that a persisting idea had emerged that somehow the problem might be approached through studying one specific area in which I myself had failed to learn something that I wanted to learn" (xviii). Failing to learn what one wants to learn is the breaking heart of creativity. Milner then admitted that her discontentment had something to do with what she had evaded, namely, trying to understand a fundamental human predicament that learning and development foster from emotional life, love, and hate.

The insight Milner would then develop for the rest of her life was a variation on the themes of love, symbolization, thinking, concentration, and reverie. For Milner, creativity would "go back to the stage before one had found a love to lose" (1990, 67). It would be a stage of orgasmic union and that, Milner argued, would set up the creative problem of communicating, giving, and receiving love. Paradoxically, the jubilant creative experience would, in and of itself, also create the conditions of inhibition and disappointment.

A surprising revelation in Milner's (1990) second edition, *On Not Being Able to Paint*, appeared late in her postscript titled "What it amounts to." Her admission, or perhaps confession, was that she wrote the introduction of her book under the cover of false confidence, as if the introduction was only following a prearranged plan. Except that the problem she was trying to express involved the situation of not learning and so any plan would be disingenuous. Even more, in thinking she was simply creating what already existed, Milner found herself "seduced by objectivity" (116). All this led Milner to question how anyone, from the beginning of life, perceives the outside world and through the creation of symbols, comes to feel the difference between inside and outside and the self and the other. How does one come to the process of reaching a semblance of objectivity through the investigation of subjectivity? Milner put the problem as one of freeing the self from the sway of an estranging "dictatorship" of exteriority (116). One consequence of her estrangement was an unwitting denial of her paintings as the symbolization of subjective life and its incompleteness. She came to the view that for the process of writing or painting to unfold, creative activity carried risks founded in the gap between the ideal and the attempt, illusion and disillusion, fusion and separateness, and even between sanity and madness. These she called "certain dangers inherent in imagination" (14). What it all amounts to for Milner is facing some rather unpleasant truths about herself and exploring the richness of the idea that "inner life is life of the body" (159).

That second edition, written after she qualified as a psychoanalyst, carried an appendix that stretched her psychoanalytic orientation to creativity into an analysis of oral and anal conflicts that affect one's relation to objects. The appendix turns more specifically to creative inhibitions and is mainly addressed to psychoanalysts: "It was clear that [my] patients had an extremely idealized notion of what their products ought to be, and the task of objective evaluation of what they in fact produced appeared to be so disillusioning to them that they gave up the attempt to produce anything" (149). Milner then speculates that the first infantile gift, received with pleasure by the mother or father, is the bowel movement. The pleasures of making a bowel movement become the model for not only that of giving but also signifies for the infant a symbolic collapse of making and giving with receiving. That is, eventually, the child understands that making shit may feel good to expel but not so good for the other to receive. Not accepting this difference may account for how often writers describe their work as 'shit.' While the infantile idealization of bodily products is required for the illusion of no separation between bodily products and externally created products, the new problem involves how love is to be given and communicated (151). There must be a separation in the form of a creation of a symbol as something other than the original thing that gave such pleasure.

What Milner thought she saw was incongruent with what she drew. The gap had to do with her question of why she set out to draw a happy scene and ended with an angry parrot. She slowly came to the view that she had angry, hostile feelings but did not see any significance in them. There was not yet a symbol or the elaboration of psychical reality. Significance for each painting would come later and mainly, she would have to pass these objects through the sieve of her doubts. And there were many. What stands out in both editions of her book, as well over the course of Milner's voluminous writings, is her capacity for revision of earlier thoughts by attending to the problems, surprises, and even cul-de-sac of symbolization. Milner thinks out loud in images; she doodles, draws, and paints in her clinical practice and considers her life projects and autobiographies as connections to ever deeper layers of association in learning and not learning.

Chapter 8 of Milner's (1990) *On Not Being Able to Paint* is titled "Preserving What One Loves." She is describing oral processes, of taking in the external world but also, the dawning idea that internalization somehow alters and even destroys the object, just as painting does. Milner then gives readers another psychical fact:

> that there might be some acute and critical moments in the history of one's power to accept, emotionally as well as intellectually, the distinction between subjective and objective, self and other, wish and what happens. And

> not only could these moments include the remembered disillusions of childhood.... There could also be other disillusionments, firmly hidden away and either actively forgotten or perhaps themselves belong to the time before the remembered years. (55)

Originally Milner (1990) set out to investigate psychic creativity, an area of existence, she felt, as disclaimed in school life and indeed, quite other to any sense of education's emphasis on cognitive progress, orderly development, and formal logic. Much later she had to wonder what the term *psychic creativity* could even mean if she could not imagine objects as both a thing and as capable of standing in for something quite other than itself. And even later with her thinking of symbols, Milner had to reconceive what she understood as "stages in objectivity" (147) just as she reconfigured her thinking on stages in perceiving subjectivity. She wrote and painted her way into the discovery of her own problems that had to do with the gap between the ideal version of what she thought a painting should be and the actual work of painting that one does. The writing of the book permitted Milner to articulate what she termed "The Facts of Art" (127) that included an understanding and acceptance of the process.

So why should an understanding and acceptance of the work of creativity be so difficult? Milner argued that it boils down to a kind of thinking. We are most used to logical thinking or giving ourselves reason, mainly to manage the innate world. Milner (1990) writes:

> We divide what we see from ourselves seeing it and in certain contexts, this works very well. But it does not work so well for understanding and managing the inner world, whether our own or other people's. (160–61)

Dissociation doesn't work so well for aesthetic engagement either. Milner eventually understood what she was facing. It was an odd dissociation from old grievances and her own sense of otherness. Only then could Milner come to an awareness of "certain dangers inherent in the imagination" (1990, 14). And this would take her into an analysis of bodily activity as our earliest experience in creating symbols for the external world, a step toward symbolic thinking. The predicament, she felt, began with the nature of illusion needed in early life—the infant's primary illusion of the union between subject and object such as that the nipple is an extension of the mouth—and the disillusion that comes from experiencing separateness, one's own otherness, and the breaking of symbolic equivalences, our earliest introduction to taking in the world that eventually can give way to the difference of symbol formation. Milner then could challenge her introduction in her postscript as her misleading habit:

> The habit of thinking in terms of purpose to deed was still so strong that when writing the introduction, after the book was nearly finished, I had almost believed that it was a true statement of how this investigation had

begun. I had almost believed that it had in fact all started with a clearly thought-out purpose; I had almost believed there had been a conscious decision that if it should be possible to settle the vague questions stimulated by the emergence of the free drawings, and to find out how to paint, then it would also be possible to answer the question of what was being left out in traditional education. But now I see that this is not true. There had been nothing in the beginning but vague uneasy feelings and an urge to follow certain trickles of curiosity wherever they might lead . . . retrospectively, that that was what I had set out to do from the beginning was an illustration of the later discovered truth that activity creates purpose. (145)

Like the painter, the writer, too, can come to the acceptance of an attitude that writing animates 'vague feelings' or traces of much earlier emotional situations that, while hardly remembered, involve experiencing separation and unity, illusion and disillusion, creation and destruction, and love and hate. Such combustible elements as emotional states do present as anxiety over how to begin while this unknowing problem becomes evaded with defenses of compliance to an introjected authority, identification with ideality, and fear of surrender to uncertainty. Constellations of argument, judgments, and frustrations occur behind the scenes for the writer and without a study of what happens within the affective frame—without a sense of our emotional ties that bind and unbind our world and their entanglements in prose and image—the writer may feel subject to haphazard melancholia, to the authority of others, and to creative flukes. All this happened to Milner when she realized that her paintings were not simply copies of reality and that the object and symbol are not the same.

To give shape to something unknown the writer does have to stretch the resin of experience into form. But how difficult that seems to be. Just as one thinks one has escaped from the dictates of common sense and schooled belief, one confronts the constraints and frames that belong to writing: choice of words, placements of ideas, writing styles, punctuation and grammar, and the shape of content.

"Ruth The Scribbler"

What of the early conflicts in creativity, namely, those Milner described as the difference between wishing to create and the more unstable and uncertain challenge made in trying to create? Here is the gap between inner reality and outer reality that Milner (1996) described in her last book, *The Suppressed Madness of Sane Men*. There she presents a short clinical snippet of "Ruth the scribbler," an eleven-year-old girl she saw in treatment.

Ruth scribbled over everything in Milner's consulting room. It looked like attacks, but Milner created another view when she wondered, what was the girl communicating to her? Milner did not begin with this question. It was asked when Milner realized her interpretations of Ruth's activities had failed. Again, Milner's approach is to study her own failures, even if it meant changing the nature of her practice, her views of what psychoanalysis should be, and her confidence in understanding. It took six months for Milner to understand Ruth's dilemma as one of expressing creativity and love:

> by refusing to discriminate and claiming the right to scribble over everything, she was trying to deny the discrepancy between the feeling and expression of it; by denying completely my right to protect any of my property from defacement she was even trying to win me over to her original belief that when she gave her messes lovingly they were literally as lovely as the feelings she had in giving them. (1996, 106)

There are two keys to Milner's thinking: first, her phrasing, "her original belief," whereby Milner imagines Ruth's infancy, and, second, the idea that creativity begins as a lovely mess prior to an interest in the difference between making and giving. In times when that distinction cannot hold or be held, the self will only express its chaotic parts as scribbles.

Scribbling may well be the first expression of desire, but for the scribbling to become a meaningful symbol, the material must be worked over. Milner ([1952] 1996) calls this fact, "a painful recognition" (107): painful because creativity requires an engagement with the frame and an awareness of the gap between intention and activity and giving and receiving. Thinking of this exchange of form as "a battle over communicating private vision," Milner arrives at the edge of her frame: "It is also a battle over the painful recognition that, if the lovely stuff is to convey the lovely feelings, there must be work done on the material" (107).

On ~~Not~~ Learning To Create

Milner often drew upon the aesthetic writing of her friend and fellow artist, Adrian Stokes. He saw artistic creation as molding a mass of material and sculpting it into new forms. Art, Stokes (2014) argued, carried on unconscious expressions of carving and resolutions in modeling. Carving, he continued, is "an attack on the material" (74). And as if to personify the act of painting, Stokes continues:

> A painter, then, to be so, must be capable of perpetrating defacement: through it be defacement in order to add, create, transform, restore, the attack is defacement none the less. The loading of the surface of the canvas, or the forcing upon this flat, white surface of an overpowering suggestion of perspective, depth, the third dimension, sometimes seems to be an enterprise not entirely dissimilar to a twisting of someone's arm. (75)

Stokes did clarify for me a difference between the writer and painter:

> It is 'seconds out of the ring' for every writer as he opposes his first unblemished sheet, innocent of his graffiti. It is even harder to paint. With the first mark or two, the canvas has become an arena in which a retaliatory bull has not yet been weakened; no substantial assault, no victory, has begun. (75)

It is the case that the vastness of the canvas, for the writer, is a mental construct. The writer tends to sit still, performs tiny gestures with the body and, turns pictures in the head into abstract words on paper. It is debatable whether every writer "is seconds out of the ring" (75). Or, if seconds out, there may follow weeks of rewriting those few seconds. For the painter, however, something so different is at stake: the image looks back, becomes its own thing, signifies a conflict between inner and outer realities, and the painter must accept the fact of painting to continue to paint. Rather than rough drafts as the writer describes, the painter creates studies of images, actions, movements, and lines of flight. One can argue that creativity is made from an interest in both destroying and rebuilding. There has to be an interest in both along with accepting the nature of the process.

We are now back to the danger of imagination, this time not as subject to inhibition but subject to the imagination itself. We can only risk a new freedom by entering uncharted relations. The violence of the creative act involves us with interpretation. In the case of the painter, there is a twisting of the image and an overturning of reality. For the writer, there can be a narrative revolt, a turning of the word and a destruction of received meaning. Psychic creativity then carries forward what is most uncertain and hopefully surprisingly novel for the work of symbolic transformation. Milner thinks of these processes as the capacity for absentmindedness, a rather radical insistence because within processes of education if we are told to be realistic, rational, and logical, we become soldiers of inhibition.

Bibliography

Farley, Lisa. 2015. "The Human Problem in Educational Research." *Curriculum Inquiry* 45 (5): 437–54.

Letley, Emma. 2014. *Marion Milner: The Life*. London: Routledge Press.

Milner, Marion. 1990. *On Not Being Able to Paint*, 2nd ed. Madison, CT: International University Press.

———. (1952) 1996. "The Role of Illusion in Symbol Formation." In *The Suppressed Madness in Sane Men: Forty-Four Years of Exploring Psychoanalysis*, 83–114. London: Routledge.

———. 1996. *The Suppressed Madness of Sane Men: Forty-Four Years of Exploring Psychoanalysis*. London: Routledge.

Stokes, Adrian. 2014. "Modes of Art and Modes of Being." In *Art and Analysis: An Adrian Stokes Reader*, edited by Meg Harris Williams, 51–78. London: Karnac Books.

CHAPTER 3

The Homoerotic Turn

IN A KEYNOTE to the Bergamo Conference on Curriculum Theory some twenty-five years ago, William Pinar surprised curriculum study with a reading of David Leavitt's (2005) novel *The Lost Language of Cranes*. With delight I recall Pinar's handling of homoerotic curriculum as a signifier for love's wagers. I imagine that if some in the audience that long-ago day were taken aback with the harshness of moral anxiety, others attached to the challenge of interpreting illegible emotional life to welcome the curriculum yet to come. Here I want to ask pressing questions: What are the stakes of the promise that gay literature can become the royal road to the knowledge of desire in education? What audacity may open education to the sotto voce of love that does speak its name and presents libidinous gay literature as curricular cathexis? Looking back on Pinar's discussion, I imagine one answer: *Read again, but this time with feeling.*

Leavitt's (2005) novel was originally published in 1986, in the midst of the North American AIDS pandemic that Paula Treichler (1988) has named as a crisis of signification, response, and care. The woeful disregard, the refusal to understand, the denial of psychical reality, and the paranoid fear remain as the manic defense mechanisms used to ward off the body and its dangers. No wonder then that Leavitt's novel drew language into the question of the loss of love and the self. As for the characters, the loss was of imagination. Leavitt's title signaled that the cranes referred not to a large, beautiful bird known for its elaborate seductions but to an ugly digging machine parked in an empty lot in a New York City neighborhood. Those machinating cranes were noisy; they invaded the ground, lifted earth, and set down its piles somewhere else. Homonyms are like that; it takes a while to reach the latent anxiety in order to restore the beauty of symbolization.

The novel asks, what is love—what is love, for whom, and with whom? One of Leavitt's main characters, called 'Phillip,' falls madly in love with Eliot, who may not really want a happy ending. Eliot has a roommate 'Jerene' who is writing her dissertation. Her topic, one of the many she begins and then abandons, is off-course. When anyone asks what the dissertation was about, Jerene preferred not to speak. Besides, there were so many topics, too many years of false starts, it is all so complicated, and then, too, there were friends who encouraged her not to finish at all. Her most recent attempt unconsciously repeats these obstacles as psychodynamics as her current study is of the child twins' phenomenon of invented language made with a condensation of sounds, secret thoughts, displacements, innuendo, and wishes for a world that both understands and does not understand. But Jerene will discuss the invented language of young girl twins. She tells both Eliot and Phillip: "I've decided to focus this chapter not on the language itself but on the response, which is in a sense more central to my thesis: what it means that a private, invented language must be scarified 'for the good of the child'" (51). Later she says, "The language had to die" (52). The novelist could be depicting what happens to most of us in education: we shed, or forget, or hide, or ignore essential being; words are treated as weapons or secret things; we have been taught to look over our shoulder; and many of us anticipate pitiful responses caught in the compulsion to repeat the damage. Pinar's stunning gift that Bergamo day invoked the right to a symbolic as the minimum condition for the right to an everyday. And the crane method that supposes all this noise and flights of movement is currere.

For those of us who have lived this homoerotic history, we may reread Leavitt's novel as a discourse on love's questions and consider our writing as a warning devise against the cruelties of repression and the illusions of normality and as our means to work through love's many blows and losses. Both the character of Phillip and his father, an academic who just walked away from his university post and took on the work of a high school guidance counselor, are gay. The son is in the midst of gay pride; the father can hardly stand himself. Phillip's mother, an editor by profession, is in an unhappy marriage. Mother, father, and son cannot speak of their desires. It is a family romance gone wrong, and as the novel slowly digs into the soft grounds of daily life, uprooting its buried disappointments and false starts, the lost language somehow makes its way back. At that long-ago keynote at Bergamo, Pinar presented these situations as currere, his method and demand for affecting autobiography interested in the destiny of its inside story projected outside to be re-transcribed through the machinations of regression, projection, and imagination. We are still learning to meet this demand, and over the years, Pinar has analyzed what holds us back with the open-ended question of what propels us forward.

What is this demand to recognize the otherness that *auto* presses into writing? One would have to be interested in the Eros of self-formation and what the gay Foucault (1988) called, in his third volume on the history of sexuality, "care of the self." Foucault, too, advises that one write from one's disciplinary regimes and consider the uses of their pleasure. One would have to delight in Roland Barthes's (2011) lectures, "The Preparation of the Novel," where he sets out the only rule with a writing phantasy:

> The principle is a general one: the subject is not to be repressed—whatever the risks to the subject.... Better the illusions of subjectivity than the impostures of objectivity. Better the Imaginary of the Subject than its censorship. (3)

Currere, after all, is a turn toward the subject, a dissonant education, akin to what Kristeva (2000) terms "narrative revolts," whereby the self is instructed by the other's questions that call upon erotic activities, active and passive positions, chance interactions, accidents, mistakes, and sundry attempts at transformation. Words are dedicated to the spirit of auscultation, free association, and transference to the ties that bind and unbind the life of the psyche.

One has to admit that education and Eros march side by side. Education has never been without gayness or its history of woeful disregard, denial of psychical reality, and the reduction of people into part objects. Most of our gay writers have their beginning in a gay childhood, and more than a few were best friends with the school librarian. I've written about the relationship between literacy and gayness and what I see today as literature provisioning the transference to a worded life (Britzman 1998). Yet even as I make this claim predicated on the emotional situation of education as containing the capacity to think more about the destiny of libido, I have in my mind a comment given by the novelist and history writer Edmund White during a 2008 book launch at one of the last standing gay-and-lesbian bookstores, Sisters, in Vancouver, British Columbia. White said that the two enemies of gay people are education and psychoanalysis. He grew up during what I think of as the bad times of ego psychology, in which psychoanalysts claimed to cure homosexuality that they attributed to a fixation of libido, regression to an earlier preoedipal state, penis envy, and dominating mothers. Why any of this made sense can only be attributed to hatred of homosexuality. All that bothered Edmund White but not so much that he stopped becoming homosexual. In a short memoir, titled "Shrinks," White (2000) began:

> In the mid 1950s, when I was fourteen or fifteen, I told my mother I was homosexual, that was the word, back then, homosexual, in its full satanic majesty, cloaked in ether fumes, a combination of evil and sickness. Of course, I'd learned the word from her. She was a psychologist. (63)

As for why education is the other enemy, one need only remember its atmosphere: the force of compliance, the loneliness of silence, the chill of coldness, and the cult of hardness tied to national mythologies that animate erotic ties and, at the same time, sever their significance. There were painful responses: the firing of teachers, hatred legislation, bad votes, public hysteria, censorship, and Anita Bryant and Roy Cohen. Yet the stories of homoeroticism in education also enact an invented language: some of us were having or imagining having sex with our teachers and schoolmates. There, in our daydreams and signs to others, love regained its wondrous name. And for a great many years, the research on sexuality in education had to dedicate itself to clearing a path, defending human rights, and looking more carefully at the aggressions in big and small education. A significant resource for such work should be literature as it has the capacity to return the repressed, this time with feeling. One need only think of Lillian Hellman's 1934 play "The Children's Hour" to take on the import of currere and the open secret that Eve Kosofsky Sedgwick (1990) named in her magnificent study of literature, "the epistemology of the closet" (67).

"For any modern question of sexuality," Sedgwick (1990) wrote, "knowledge/ignorance is more than merely one in a metonymic chain of such binarisms" (73). One can state this with feeling: there can be no signifier without sexuality and phantasy. Around 1989 and, I think, due to those in literature and language departments—recall the mothers of inventions: Teresa de Lauretis, Eve Kosofsky Sedgwick, and Judith Butler. Their idea of queer theory served as the means for the analysis of the subject of language. For many of us, this enigmatic frame contained our justified anger for what has happened in failed education. I was inspired to write the paper "Is There a Queer Pedagogy? Or, Stop Reading Straight" (Britzman 1995). That title now reads as schizoid. At the time, that was how I felt: bifurcated, split, and alienated. The reparation, I felt, could only come from reading otherwise. So I posed the question of reading practices along with their inhibitions and leaned on the work of Cindy Patton (1990), whose focus was on the splitting mechanisms of us versus them; Sedgwick (1990), who considered the reparative uses of a universalizing discourse; and Shoshana Felman's (1987) discussion of pedagogy as embroiled in what Lacan has named as our passion for ignorance. They inspired the queer reading practice of implication and the capacity for new subject positions. My demand for a queer pedagogy was also an attempt to grapple with the terms of heteronormativity, a rather clunky word that signified an invasive phantasy, mistaken yet dangerous. However awkward, the word gave us a foothold into questions: What is normal, and why do we care? But as a catchword, more often than not, it became a sort of accusation and in this sense, repeated hostility, persecutory guilt, and splitting mechanisms. It was like turning the tables, although not yet an interpretation in the psychoanalytic sense of calling for free association, linking, and new narratives.

Pinar's (1998) edited collection "Queer Theory in Education" reminds us that if queers are hardly strangers to the constitution of pedagogy—that more than shadow play occurred in Plato's cave—at the time of the publication of his edited volume, and now looking back at it, no unity could be established amidst its authors as to what is really queer about queer theory. I believe the same question circulates in the psychoanalytic field, and we must have the audacity to ask again, What is psychoanalytic about psychoanalysis? Can we read queer theory with psychoanalysis to exceed our well-schooled pedagogical principles and welcome our desire to freely associate with curriculum? Pinar's (1998) reply: "One might then think of identities and sexualities as formed and reformed through *fantasized acts of relationality*" (27, italics added).

Are we ready for phantasy? This is the direction I have entered with the psychoanalytic idea that education can recommend an interest in psychical reality with an affectionate theory of learning capable of containing anxiety and addressing our emotional situations of changing minds in teaching and learning (Britzman 2015). For example, consider theories of Melanie Klein, who, after all, seems to extend Barthes's measure—"better the illusions of the imaginary"—to the furthest reaches of psychical life. Klein brings us into the intimate chaos of phantasy, thought of as an unconscious constellation of drives, anxieties, and defenses, that paradoxically are the soft foundation for symbolization. For Klein—and her theory was worked out with very young children at play with 'toy people'—phantasy is a function of the mind, its contents, its mechanisms, and its means for handling the difference between internal reality and the external world. It begins, however, in frustration of weaning and the loss of the breast that somehow creates movement from the terror of part objects to the apperception of whole people, expressed in the oscillation between the paranoid-schizoid and depressive positions. Phantasy, to say the least, is a felt experience of extremity and excess and, step by step, leads to the capacity to hold the object in mind without recourse to hostility, denial of psychical reality, and the hardening of the early defenses of omnipotence, projective identification, and persecutory anxiety (Britzman 2016). Many years ago, I would not have associated the work of currere to the working through of the depressive position, but the sequence, something Freud ([1914] 1968) first saw in one of his early technique papers as "remembering, repeating, and working through" and what Klein would then see as the freeing of phantasies for imagination and a more capacious sense of reality as interpreted reality, is similar in hopes. But for Klein ([1935] 1975), one must pass through the object relations: imagos of anxiety, aggression, and defense and then as worries over the destruction of the object.

On the way to Klein ([1935] 1975), it is worth quoting Freud on such matters:

> We have learnt that the patient repeats instead of remembering, and repeats under the conditions of resistance.... [H]e repeats everything that has already made its way from the sources of the repressed into his manifest personality. ... He also repeats all his symptoms in the course of the treatment ... the compulsion to repeat. (151)

And Klein would see the repetition compulsion as the hostile denial of the significance of psychical reality. Her contribution was that she took this hostility as only the beginning of transference.

Should we introject the homoerotic object, complications emerge. The conflicts have much to do with the vulnerability of self-love, abandoned when the self is diminished and when love of the other is unacknowledged. David Leavitt's (2005) novel, perhaps not the great gay novel, although one of many that calls upon the intimacies and failures of learning and response, is unafraid to narrate earlier states of defense, such as omnipotence and splitting, and link them to aggressive drives. What would have to be analyzed, then, are the anxieties of influence and introjection rooted in the underlying guilt of a superego that must destroy the good object. In so doing, the ego shatters. Klein argued that for the consciousness of right and wrong to be apprehended and acted upon the superego must become diminished in its commands. But it all stems from the capacity for guilt, needed for reparation and gratitude.

Klein has argued that symbolization is our second chance to love. Love is the greatest defense against diminishing the inner world, and in trying to sustain the good object, anxiety is justified, though just the beginning. Klein ([1935] 1975) gave notice to an emotional sense of the difficulties wrought by the urgency of fragmentation:

> There is anxiety how to put the bits together in the right way and at the right time; how to pick out the good bits and do away with the bad ones; how to bring the object to life when it has been put together; and there is the anxiety of being interfered with in this task by bad objects and by one's own hatred, etc. Anxiety situations of this kind I have found to be at the bottom of not only depression, but of all inhibitions of work. (269–70)

I can only be schematic in my attempt to suggest the fragility of the homoerotic turn for it begins life. My hunch is that whether we begin with currere or psychoanalysis, curriculum study as a view of life now has the difficult task of moving from the depressive anxiety to a creative position, one unafraid of human vulnerability as both the bare element of the human condition and the place from which we write. The proposal would be to recommend the homoerotic turn, just as we must recommend apprehension of psychical reality. And the phantasy demand would go something like this: *Read again, but this time with feeling.*

Bibliography

Barthes, Roland. 2011. *The Preparation of the Novel: Lecture Courses and Seminars at the Collège de France (1978–1979 and 1979–1980).* Translated by Kate Briggs. New York: Columbia University Press.

Britzman, Deborah P. 1995. "Is There a Queer Pedagogy? Or, Stop Reading Straight." *Educational Theory* 45 (2): 151–66.

———. 1998. *Lost Subjects, Contested Objects: Toward a Psychoanalytic Inquiry of Learning.* Albany: State University of New York Press.

———. 2015. *A Psychoanalyst in the Classroom: On the Human Condition of Education.* Albany: State University of New York Press.

———. 2016. *Melanie Klein: Early Analysis, Play, and the Question of Freedom.* London: Springer Press.

Felman, Shoshana. 1987. *Jacques Lacan and the Adventure of Insight: Psychoanalysis in Contemporary Culture.* Cambridge, MA: Harvard University Press.

Foucault, M. 1988. *The Care of the Self.* Translated by Robert Hurley. New York: Vintage Books.

Freud, Sigmund. (1914) 1968. "Remembering, Repeating and Working-Through (Further Recommendations on the Technique of Psycho-Analysis II)." In *The Standard Edition of the Complete Psychological Works of Sigmund Freud, Volume XII (1911–1913): The Case of Schreber, Papers on Technique and Other Works*, edited and translated by James Strachey, in collaboration with Anna Freud, 145–56. London: Hogarth Press.

Klein, Melanie. (1935) 1975. "A Contribution to the Psychogenesis of Manic-Depressive States." In *Love, Guilt, and Reparation, and Other Works, 1921–1945*, 262–89. London: Hogarth Press.

Kristeva, Julia. 2000. *The Sense and Non-Sense of Revolt: The Powers and Limits of Psychoanalysis, Vol. 1.* Translated by Jeanine Herman. New York: Columbia University Press.

Leavitt, David. 2005. *The Lost Language of Cranes.* New York: Bloomsbury.

Patton, Cindy. 1990. *Inventing AIDS*. New York: Routledge Press.
Pinar, William. 1998. "Introduction." In *Queer Theory in Education*, edited by William Pinar, 1–49. Mahwah, NJ: Lawrence Erlbaum Associates.
Sedgwick, Eve Kosofsky. 1990. *Epistemology of the Closet*. Berkeley: University of California Press.
Treichler, Paula A. 1988. "AIDS, Homophobia, and Biomedical Discourse: An Epidemic of Signification." In *AIDS: Cultural Analysis, Cultural Activism*, edited by Douglas Crimp, 31–71. Boston: MIT Press.
White, Edmund. 2000. "Shrinks." *Granta* 71 (1): 61–90.

CHAPTER 4

Teacher Education In The Confusion of Our Times

IF IT IS a truism that in order to teach, teachers must engage knowledge, it is also right to observe that as this new century unfolds, there is still little agreement in our field of teacher education as to which knowledge matters or even what might be the matter with knowledge. Nor is there much understanding over how those trying to teach actually learn from their practices, their students, or their incidental anxieties made from acquiring experience. We cannot agree on the length of the practicum, on whether the nineteenth-century apprentice model is still relevant, or even on imagining the future of schooling itself. Various learning taxonomies developed over the twentieth century try to settle these doubts, yet, however elaborated or simplified, the measures on offer never seem adequate to the uncertainties made from teaching and learning. It is difficult, then, to even find the subject of teacher education, so inundated is our field with the romance of cognitive styles, the rumblings of brain research, the idealization of information and standards, and the parade of new diagnosis of learning failures: attention-deficit disorders, overstimulation, under-stimulation, and not enough Mozart. At the close of the twentieth century, in the confusion of our times, we seem to have a better idea of all that we lack than we do of what makes understanding so difficult (Britzman 1998) or even how we might think about the psychological significance of teacher education.

We do know more about what holds education and teacher education back. There is the force of governmental interdictions, censoring both ideas and the personal lives of teachers and students. Our own definitions of professionalism preclude complications of selves and then ask for compliance and conformity. We have made great strides in emptying the curriculum from debating itself. Symptoms of these maladies can be observed: camera surveillance devices, weapon detectors, and corporate ID tags for students and teachers. Behind these symptoms is the stultifying dream of uniting the nation through a common curriculum, made safe from any controversy. And then we are caught in a repetitive debate over whether schools and teacher education can or should be able to prevent eruptions of social violence. The old question of what schooling is for becomes utterly entangled with what it means to think about school and teacher education as part and parcel in the world. Somewhere between the dream of education and its nightmare of the daily grind, we lose and find teacher education.

Profound disagreement over preparation, not just how to prepare teachers but also how schools prepare students, mirrors contemporary global themes. However, nowhere does this question of what one should know and how knowledge might matter take on more poignancy than when nations decide to confront and work through their own buried pasts of human devastations and genocide. Simply put, if we can bear to learn from history, all that we know about history requires reconstruction, not just of texts and contexts but also ourselves, of an intimate identity and what might be included under the name 'potential.' From the South African Truth Commission, in where victims and perpetrators faced each other, to the failed Israeli/Palestinian Peace Accords; from the house arrest in London of Chilean general Pinochet and the Chilean courts decision to bring to trial those previously granted amnesty, to the art exhibit in Columbia called "Art and Violence in Colombia since 1948" that calls citizens to confront the nation's demise; from the spate of national apologies, in the case of the United States for enslaving Africans and in the case of the pope, for the history of anti-Semitism in Catholic liturgy, to the problem of present responsibilities; and from renewed discussions on Germany's reunion and the move of its capital city back to Berlin to new and more devastating acknowledgments of the reach of the Shoah in our own times, the violence of the national repressed returns what Caruth (1996) named as "unclaimed experience." These are all pedagogical projects, not of management but of thinking and revising thought. How is it that so much of our past century remains unclaimed in education? And how can teacher education come to make itself relevant to such ethical obligations? If teacher education could begin to reclaim difficult knowledge what would be the work of teacher educators?

All these events should remind us of our present implication in world-making catastrophes. Felman's (1992) difficult question might allow us to rethink the confusions of our times:

> In a post-traumatic century, a century that has survived unthinkable historical catastrophes, is there anything that we have learned or that we should learn about education that we did not know before? (1)

One might be tempted to dismiss Felman's question as just another burden, yet another agenda. Our oldest educational complaint, after all, is that there is not enough time to address existential, political, or even ontological breakdown. Yet what is it that we do with our time that we can do without these difficulties? If we take Felman seriously, crisis inaugurates the work of education, even as education makes new forms of crisis. However, when one looks at what counts as a crisis in teacher education, the world shrinks: its geography is rather stingy, its disciplinary borrowings rather mere, its reliance upon social sciences as the knowledge base shameful, its eschewal of what is old-fashionably called 'the mysteries of psychical life,' or the strange and unmastered ways we are subject to unconscious phantasies, sad. Left unasked is the question of how teacher education becomes psychologically significant, giving way to its participants to explore the uncertainties of freedom and passion. A tiny sense of teacher education speaks volumes of our woeful disregard of the fragility of learning and of knowledge in our present; lost is the capacity to expand the reach and relevancy in our field, and our thinking of how teacher education can come to matter to those involved.

Undoubtedly, these are all big issues. The little issues matter as well and are made from daily encounters of selves facing one another in a classroom and the ways each of us are as susceptible to our perceptions as we are to what we ignore and to that which we cannot bear to know. Indeed, the intimate problems of how one becomes affected by knowledge, by the experiences of strangers, and by histories that are not our own, not in terms of its application for others but in terms of our own capacities to affect and be touched by knowledge, remains one of the grand paradoxes of our new century. Usually, our disillusion with the promise of knowledge and progress is raised from the ruins of tremendous social breakdown and from the difficulties of understanding what went so terribly wrong. The philosopher Theodor Adorno, for example, wondered what education could be after Auschwitz. He came to this difficult question because of his work in teacher education: When World War II ended, Adorno, who was in exile in the United States, returned to Germany. His chief means of employment upon return was in a teachers' college where he was assigned the charge of examining secondary teachers on the topic of philosophy (Hohendahl 1995). Adorno (1998) noticed that while the candidates could give adequate answers, they also admitted that philosophy meant nothing to them. They passed the exam by offering clichéd accounts and platitudes:

> This test therefore should permit us to see whether those candidates, who as teachers in secondary schools are burdened with a heavy responsibility for the spiritual and material development of Germany, are intellectuals, or, as Ibsen said more than eighty years ago, merely specialized technicians. (21)

Critical pedagogy in North America would also raise such concerns, wondering whether teacher education might exceed the normative cloak of professionalism and, instead, inspire itself to be unafraid to ask new kinds of questions and to receive questions that break open rigid preconceptions of our field.

Hannah Arendt (1993) also centered the theme of crisis in education. Just as Felman (1992) insisted that education is crisis, before her, Arendt elaborated the stakes:

> Which aspects of the modern world and its crisis have actually revealed themselves in the educational crisis. . . . What can we learn from this crisis for the essence of education—not in the sense that one can always learn from mistakes what ought not to be done, but rather by reflecting on the role that education plays in every civilization, that is on the obligation that the existence of children entails for every human society. (184–85)

Arendt asked educators to assume a certain dignity within vulnerability, that children were becoming adults but that they were already, like adults, humans. Arendt did not mean that we are all the same or that there is an original innocence that adults must preserve. Instead, she wanted us to consider something difficult: the meeting of adults and children as an ethical obligation yet to be accomplished.

We can raise a similar question for teacher education: What are our obligations, not in the sense of getting work done but in the way we imagine our work and how our workings affect our capacity to think beyond what we do? What inhibits our capacity to respond ethically to others, to learn something from people we will never meet, and to be affected by histories that we may never live? Can teacher education create conditions for all of us to risk the self in an encounter with histories of bad faith? If we can take seriously the thinking of people like Arendt, Adorno, and Felman, we might wonder why education has such difficulty with encountering its own breakdowns, blind spots, and vulnerabilities. We have yet to grapple with what knowledge does to teachers, particularly, the difficult knowledge of social catastrophe, evidence of woeful disregard, experiences of social violence, illness, and death, and, most generally, with what it means to come to terms with various kinds of trauma, individual and collective. What makes trauma traumatic is the incapacity to respond adequately, accompanied by feelings of profound helplessness and loss, and a sense that no other person or group will intervene. What makes trauma traumatic is the loss of self and other.

World making requires interest in what the world might symbolize or represent for the self. The self is both our earliest and oldest technology. This first obligation to 'know thyself' brings to the fore the little matters of teacher education, not just because it might take us away from the romance of technology, the rubble of the information highway, and the illusions made from the testing industry, although this would be enough. The work of knowing the self entails acknowledging not just what one would like to know about the self but also what is difficult to know about the self, including features we tend to project to others: aggression, self-aggrandizement, destructive wishes, and helplessness. These are the devastating qualities of psychical life. And yet something about education resists self-knowledge.

What happens to the self who teaches? Gardner (1997, 3) offers one of the more honest formulations: all we can do is try to teach but this effort often gets caught in the tangles of what he calls, "the true teacher's defining affliction: furor to teach" (3). By this, he means forgetting the students or teaching in spite of them, maybe even to spite them. He also means that just as when we believe in the knowledge we offer students, there is a centripetal tendency to freeze knowledge by undervaluing our questioning of it and forgetting the importance of doubting the very knowledge on offer. The furor to teach defends against this capacity to doubt and the interest in using knowledge as a means for world and self-making.

This is not the first time the manic defense of teaching was noticed. At the beginning of this century, when William James lectured to Harvard's future teachers in 1899, he dedicated many lectures to the aggressive qualities of what can only be called the 'full-speed-a-head' school of teaching. Warning teachers against their habituated thinking, their automatic associations, their unconscious wishes, and what he called "a certain blindness in human beings," James asked his audience to ponder their own obstacles to thought and how these obstacles structured their actions of teaching and learning in his last lecture, "What Makes Life Significant":

> In my previous talk, "On a Certain Blindness," I tried to make you feel how soaked and shot-through life is with values and meanings which we fail to realize because of our external and insensible point of view. The meanings are there for the others, but they are not there for us. There lies more than a mere interest of curious speculation in understanding this. I wish that I could convince you of it as I feel it myself. It is the basis of all our tolerance, social religious, and political. The forgetting of it lies at the root of every stupid and sanguinary mistake that rulers over subject-people make. (150)

Anna Freud's ([1930] 1974) four lectures to teachers on psychoanalysis would also offer comparable warnings, noting a certain blindness toward and defense against exploring the vulnerabilities of the interior life. Her first lecture begins with an observation that still holds in our own time: "We are all aware that teachers are still very suspicious and doubtful of psychoanalysis" (73). Nonetheless, over the course of her four lectures, she tries to offer particular frames for interpreting not so much the dream of education but what the dream defends against: rescue fantasies, altruistic surrender, hostility toward the student, the eschewal of the reach of sexuality, and the difficulties of remembering one's own childhood researches. Her last lecture also suggests why teachers may be suspicious of psychoanalysis:

> Probably you seek practical advice rather than extension of theoretical knowledge.... Above all, you want to know whether we, as adults, should interfere more or be less authoritarian than adults have been in the past. The answer to the last question I have to say that psychoanalysis so far has stood for limiting the efforts of education by emphasizing some specific dangers connected with it. (123)

Anna Freud left the audience to decide not only which dangers mattered, but also what might be the matter with their own teacher education.

James (1899) and A. Freud (1930) noticed a difficulty in learning from ideas that rattle not just the learner but also the very foundations of education. Adam Phillips (1998) offers an even more radical principle for what we might encounter as education. What would education be like if our attention was given over to "the irregular, to the oddity, the unpredictability of what each person makes of what he is given—the singularity born of each person's distinctive history. The sense in which a passionate life is a good life because of its goodness is always in question" (40–41). What allows for the possibility of distinct histories is the effort in questioning one's own narratives. How then are questions made?

According to Winnicott (1996), questions are made from our doubts and our defenses against doubt. To illustrate this, he analyzes the stakes of a common question, "Yes, but is it true?"

Winnicott (1996) was struggling with how students began to learn from their study of psychology. He noted two stages in trying to learn from the mysteries of psychical life, from how one feels torn by new and old knowledge. At first, students tended to see the knowledge of psychology strictly in terms of how they can apply it to others, a form of compliance with the knowledge and with the tacit cultural value that knowledge must be useable. Gardner (1997) may have had in mind such a conflict with his notion, 'the furor to teach.' The second stage of learning is destructive in the sense that all learning must be destructive; along with trying to make psychology one's own, the student will criticize, raise questions, doubt it, and if the knowledge can survive this attack, it can be turned inward toward the self. Where Phillips (1998) places our capacity to question the goodness of our narratives, Adorno (1998) situates a heavy responsibility. Both Winnicott and Phillips, however, argue that self-knowledge comes after the self experiences. Self-knowledge is not a feature of the experience but a residue of the self's desire to keep the experience as his or her own, to feel once again one's affective ties, to remind the self that ideas one did know before, can now matter.

What if teacher education began with such a simple model of learning? Could there be a movement from self-knowledge to world making? We would have to think about how the teaching techniques we offer induce compliance in the form of our students quickly taking techniques into their classrooms. This rush to application and to what mistakenly is called 'practical' would, of course, be only compliance to the dominant rule that knowledge use is strictly defined by its capacity to be externalized and applied to others. It will take time to notice the qualities of ideas at stake, not from the vantage of the triumph of application but from the difficulties of describing what James (1899) named as 'habituated knowledge' and what Arendt (1993) called 'ethical obligations.' To implicate oneself in one's own narratives of learning and teaching means turning habituated knowledge back upon itself and examining its most unflattering, indeed, for many, its most devastating features. It also means exploring how even this most unflattering moment may offer insight into making significance.

There is nothing easy about encountering histories of woeful disregard. At the end of our twentieth century, teacher education has yet to acknowledge the confusion of our times and the defense of confusion that is used to give up on learning. Learning from the other's trauma is of a different order, one where the application of knowledge is irrelevant because knowledge of trauma is other to the knowledge of mastery, application, and standardization. This does not mean traumatic knowledge cannot be worked through. However, it does mean that many of the arguments in our field are irrelevant to new ways of conceptualizing our worldly obligations. If teacher education is to join the world, be affected by its participation in world making, and question the 'goodness' of its own passions, we must not only rethink past practices and what goes on under the name of professionalism but also create the very imagination needed to exceed compliance, fear of controversy, and 'unclaimed experiences.' Then, we might ask a new question: How does teacher education come to notice that the world matters?

Bibliography

Adorno, Theodor W. 1998. *Critical Models: Interventions and Catchwords*. Translated by H. Pickford. New York: Columbia University Press.

Arendt, Hannah. 1993. *Between Past and Future: Eight Exercises in Political Thought*. New York: Penguin Books.

Britzman, Deborah. P. 1998. *Lost Subjects, Contested Objects: Toward a Psychoanalytic Inquiry of Learning*. Albany: State University of New York Press.

Caruth, Cathy. 1996. *Unclaimed Experience: Trauma, Narrative, and History*. Baltimore, MD: Johns Hopkins University Press.

Felman, Shoshana. 1992. "Education and Crisis, or the Vicissitudes of Teaching." In *Testimony: Crises of Witnessing in Literature, Psychoanalysis, and History*, edited by Shoshana Felman and Dori Laub, 1–56. New York: Routledge.

Freud, Anna. (1930) 1974. "Four Lectures on Psychoanalysis for Teachers and Parents." In *The Writings of Anna Freud 1922–35 Vol. 1 Introduction to Psychoanalysis and Lectures for Child Analysts and Teachers*, 73–137. New York: International Universities Press.

Gardner, Robert M. 1994. *On Trying to Teach: The Mind in Correspondence*. Hillsdale, NJ: The Analytic Press.

Hohendahl, Peter U. 1995. *Prismatic Thought: Theodor W. Adorno*. Lincoln: University of Nebraska Press.

James, William. (1899) 1983. *Talks to Teachers on Psychology and to Students on Some of Life's Ideals*. Cambridge, MA: Harvard University Press.

Phillips, Adam. 1998. *The Beast in the Nursery: On Curiosity and Other Appetites*. New York: Pantheon Books.

Winnicott, Donald W. (1950) 1996. "Yes, But How Do We Know It's True?" In *Thinking about Children*, edited by Ray Shepherd, Jennifer Johns, and Helen Taylor Robinson, 13–18. Reading, MA: Addison-Wesley.

CHAPTER 5

On Some Psychical Consequences of AIDS Education

IN MY EXPLORATIONS of the psychical consequences of learning, I have been wondering about pedagogy's capacity to address the ego (Britzman 1998). This project renders as curious pedagogy's current preoccupation with making the proper curriculum that can somehow prop up the coherence of knowledge and its subjects. The detour moves from a pedagogy preoccupied with knowledge to one that attempts a dialogue with psychical dynamics of learning, with the failure of knowledge, and then a move toward what Jacqueline Rose (1993) terms an "ethics of failure" (36) that have to do with attempts to do less harm in social, ontological, and epistemological breakdown.[1] Here, I suggest the relevancy of new conceptualizations for AIDS education. For even as we attempt to offer less damaging information and ready ourselves to rethink current representations of the virus, its global trajectory, medical interventions, at-risk bodily practices, and community campaigns, we also know those appeals to a rational, cohesive, and unitary subject in the name of toleration, role models, and the affirmation of and reliance on identity return the damage. Whereas those who do attempt to assist students in a creative and ethical engagement with the study of AIDS already know the difficulties in terms of subject, object, and conceptual reformulations demanded and in terms of institutional and legal prohibitions against frank discussion and uncensored texts, the *little* difficulty involves what it might mean for a pedagogy to attempt to address the ego's work of making reparation in learning and unlearning.

Why be preoccupied with the ego? What is the ego that it should become the destination of a pedagogical address? From the writing of Freud (1923), and then, those who follow after, we learn that the ego is first of all a bodily ego, a "frontier-creature" (56) whose work is perception, judgment, defense, and reality testing. We learn as well that the ego attempts to synthesize that which cannot be resolved, namely the estranging relations between psychical dynamics and social demands. Here is the most intimate expression of the failure of knowledge. Furthermore, we learn that because of the ego's desire to synthesize and the impossibility of fleeing from itself when things, inevitably, do not work out, as that great seat of anxiety the ego has special methods called defense mechanisms that are put to work in order for the ego to live through its interminable conflicts. Freud complicates the picture even more in his portrayal of the ego as tragic. The ego's defense mechanisms are formed at a time when the ego is just emerging, too young really, to understand that in its lonely attempts to defend itself, to differentiate itself from its own anxieties, it will set in motion the very dilemmas it desires to flee. Perhaps this is why in his defense of lay analysis, Freud called the ego 'feeble.' In a rather condensed discussion of the flawed ego, Freud (1926b) suggests that the work of the ego can cause it to fall ill:

> The point at which the illness makes its breach is an unexpected one, though no one acquainted with general pathology will be surprised to find a confirmation of the principle that is precisely the most important developments and differentiations that carry in them the seeds of illness, the failure of function. (202)[2]

The work of the ego places the ego at risk. Freud argued something more, and here is where education matters. Although Freud acknowledged the ego's loyalty to the world, a loyalty that tends to spin the ego against the 'it' or the 'id' of itself and that tends toward the wish for an absolute knowledge and unification, he supposed that the forces at work within the ego also push the ego to change the world as opposed to simply adapting to and complying with its demands. Although education also has this same constitutional ambivalence in its attempt to distinguish between change and adaptation, a more intimate movement tends to be ignored. For Melanie Klein (1994) the movement is love as "the desire to make reparation." I think we need to invoke the fragile potential of the ego to make reparation and discuss why pedagogy must attempt an address to this other learning with a deep understanding of 'ethics of failure.'

A series of sentences, phrases, and footnotes serve as a guide.

First the sentences: for Sigmund Freud, I can offer you no consolation; for Anna Freud, we should not expect so much of each other. Whereas Freud promises nothing, Anna Freud considers the promise to be too harsh, for the expectation is always anxious. They both address the ego as the great seat of anxiety that must console itself and as that great possibility for a movement toward risking its own history of love. In this dreamy history, knowledge will always be fragile, subject to reversal, displacement, substitution, and condensation. The ego is a precipitate of its own libidinal history, its capacity to touch and be touched. This libidinal history, although never fully conscious, nonetheless exerts great force. Yet if the ego is an effect of love, if the ego is to be affected by its own love, Freud ([1932] 1933) goes on to suggest another potential, a queer relation that may be of interest to educators: "Where id was, there ego shall be" (80). Suppose, then, that pedagogy could attend to the time of delay noted by the two Freuds. For this to occur, pedagogy would have to address what Erik Erikson (1968), in his discussion of classroom life calls, "a communality of egos" (221) and then incite something in excess of what Hanns Sachs (1947) in his consideration of literature calls, "a community of daydreams" (281).[3]

If pedagogy can reside in the fault line of these sentences and phrases—promising nothing, not expecting so much—it might begin again with another sentence of delay, the time that inaugurates Sarah Schuman's (1990) novel *People in Trouble*: "It was the beginning of the end of the world but not everyone noticed right away" (1). We know that in the field of education, not everyone notices right away. And if one attempted to write the history of AIDS in educational discourse, by which I mean if one could study contemporary responses to the pandemic known as AIDs in that place where the masses of people in North America are legally mandated to go, one would have to begin by writing stories of the woeful disregard toward the events known as AIDS and notice how even such tiny and intimate objects like condoms and safer-sex pamphlets can contribute to a school district's hysteria, to the cruelness of social policy, and to the passion for prohibitions.[4] We might also notice the silence of teacher education. These add up to a story of obscurantism, the withholding of knowledge, and a confining of what Driscilla Cornell (1995) terms "the imaginary domain," or the right to imagine something otherwise. This disregard, a disavowal, would be, in Shoshana Felman's (1987) terms, a story of ignorance, a story rooted in the desire to ignore. Even this desire would also be a story of stunning implication, entangled in what Jonathan Silin (1995) argues as one that "radically calls into question the pleasures and dangers of teaching" (56). The pleasure and the danger have to do not just with how knowledge is used but the very poesies of its in-betweenness, namely, the social relations of cultural experience, play, and the creative work where Winnicott (1986) locates the potential space as opening the question of freedom.

If pedagogy can ready itself to question such a radical call—a call that would ask for an account of its pleasures and dangers—it must also admit to its tally: symptoms of not noticing right away. For in education, the story of AIDS would resemble a symptom-formation, a defense against noticing. Freud's (1926b) description is a shocking reversal:

> The symptom-formation scores a triumph if it succeeds in combining the prohibition with satisfactions so that what was originally a defensive command, or prohibition acquires the significance of a satisfaction as well; and in order to achieve this end it will often make use of the most ingenious associative paths. (112)

One such pathway in education is made from obsessive worry about invoking controversy. The controversy belongs not to any topic but to a history of ignorance. We would have to understand how education gains satisfaction in the story of woeful disregard. Freud (1926b) called this resistance, "the gain from illness" (223). Much later, Christopher Bollas (1992) would call this refusal, "the violence of innocence" (165).[5]

And yet this story of woeful disregard may not explain why Bill Haver (1996) writes, "Not even education can save us now" (23). The sentence is not just a warning about educational mythology and its passionate identification with the rescue fantasy, with the idealization of the good object and then with having to split the ego so that what becomes unthinkable is what Klein ([1937]1975) calls "making reparation" (311). Haver's warning marks the limits of a certain education. Yet marking the limit is not the same as experiencing it. Again, Schulman (1990) writes, "It was the beginning of the end of the world but not everyone noticed right away" (1).

What then is it to notice? And why is not noticing so common? We can turn to a different sort of warning offered by analyst Alice Balint (1954): "Education begins at an age at which it is too early for us to be able to count on understanding" (119). Balint's concern is not with the bringing up of culture as the bildungsroman of the educational romance. Nor can her observation be consoled through the progress of chronology and its promise of maturity. The story of regression should bother our attempts at cure. Balint marks the strange time of learning as *too early, too late, belated*. If education cannot count on understanding—after all, learning is only a movement toward what is not yet understood or perhaps even tolerated—then on what can pedagogy count? It must count on the question of not understanding, of misrecognition, and only from these flaws may come a possibility and desire to make reparation. Before leaving these fragments of delay, let us consider why a theory of delay in learning is of some psychical consequence.

Balint posits the ego's work of perception as contributing to its own circumscription. She calls this first flawed attempts at learning *identificatory thought*. Balint defines this way of thinking as the ego's attempt to make a relation to the world while still desiring both to console its own impossible defense of omnipotence and as its means to ward off the fear of annihilation. But the very attempt is doomed because identificatory thought is so closely linked to the ego's primary narcissism and hence identification does not mean to distinguish or tolerate difference. In Balint's (1954) words, "identificatory thinking is employed for the purpose of avoiding what is unpleasurable and obtaining what is pleasurable, and it aims at transforming a strange and consequently frightening external world into one that is familiar an enjoyable" (93). Identificatory thought is a symptom of the ego's capacity to hallucinate. And, for Balint, identificatory thought is a strategy of resistance, not yet love. In Balint's terms, the lover must tolerate the vicissitudes of the loved object and find pleasure in the unfamiliar.

Those of us who attempt to open curriculum to studies of AIDS know that many students may prefer their own resistance and when introduced, these students may wish for the teacher's removal. Indeed, identificatory thinking may well be a defense against the unpleasure of confronting oneself when facing one's attitudes toward learning from AIDS. And yet the common cruel statements that accompany the refusal to learn, the dismissal of the learning, and the desire to ignore may not easily map onto conscious meanings or even invoke any insight into the latent content of resistance. Resistance is not transparent; its very qualities refuse its own unveiling. Freud ([1924] 1925) suggests resistance will show up in two ways: "as critical objection and through allusive approximations... more remote from the actual idea" (41).[6] Because resistance is carried within so many interminable disguises and essentially repeats the logic of dream-work through condensation, distortion, reversal of content, and so on, as a symptom formation, meeting resistance requires interpretation rather than moral judgment. Even if the resistance is interpreted well by an outsider, it is still the resister who must become willing to risk her or his own satisfaction with not learning. Appeals to rationality are of no help because the defenses at work are built on anxiety. For this reason, education occurs at a time when it is too early for us to count on anyone's understanding, including the educator.

So too with the defense of repression, one of the ego's special methods "to struggle against painful or unendurable ideas or affects" (A. Freud [1936] 1995, 42). There are two ego defense strategies that are central when considering why a pedagogy of AIDS is so fragile: the mechanism of 'undoing what has been done' and 'isolation.' Sigmund Freud (1926a) calls 'undoing' a negative magic because it is not just the consequences that must be ignored. The event itself is 'blown away.' A person decides an event did not happen, a kind of denial of denial. Isolation is the second defense, whereby, although the event is acknowledged, the individual decides it will not matter: "the event is deprived of its affect, and its associative connections are suppressed or interrupted so that it remains as though isolated and is not reproduced in the ordinary process of thought" (120). One does not have to go very far to suggest that isolation of affect and idea and undoing what has already happened may be the key structure in educational design and authority.[7] But these defense mechanisms impoverish thinking. This is partly because undoing and isolation refuse any obligation to implicate the self in what is there but not noticed. A well-meaning pedagogy cannot predict how or when its address is felt as a threat or as too much. Here, pedagogy cannot be in mastery of itself and like the ego subjects itself, without noticing, to its own symptoms, anxieties, and defenses.

Curiously, the mechanisms of undoing and isolation appear rational in structure while requiring conviction for a flawed logic oriented toward the view that knowledge and bodies are capable of securing their own boundaries. Freud (1926a) proposes the roots of undoing and isolation harken back to an archaic taboo against touching. We are, of course, back to the question of AIDS and the ego's tragic defense against being touched by AIDS. In Freud's words,

> [i]f we ask ourselves why the avoidance of touching, contact, or contagion should play such a large part in this neurosis and should become the subject-matter of complicated systems, the answer is that touching and physical contact are the immediate aim of the aggressive as well as the loving object-cathexes. Eros desires contact. (122)

There are two sorts of touching. One is aggressive touching as a paradox of hatred: a touch made in order to not be touched. The other is loving, for this touch is without condition, cannot guarantee, and only desires. The loving touch is vulnerable to loss; these the ego must risk in order to love. The aggressive touch is already one of loss that is not known. Both aggressive and loving touching, in Klein's terms, must be engaged, for if the subject does not come to notice her own capacity to do harm—including her capacity to do conceptual violence—there can be no desire to make reparation.

We can begin to see that AIDS education makes difficult demands on communities of egos: let go of defenses, be touched by that which puts you in danger, change conceptual and affective resistances, and acknowledge something more than your fears. This potential space is where thinking might move toward an ethical relation and engage its potential to become contaminated, wounded by thought. This ethical turn refuses the boundaries of certitude and properness to permit the ego's encounter with its original own demand to love and to be loved.

So far, I have been considering questions of disavowal, withdrawal, and with the ambivalence of touching and being touched. I suggested that these intimate dynamics are repeated at the level of the social and its ingested meanings. The other side is also difficult. What renders AIDS education insufficient is that we do not know the subject of AIDS. We have yet to learn from AIDS a lesson in the failure of the calculations of knowledge.[8] In Haver's (1996) words,

> [w]hat is called AIDS poses an essential threat not only to our commonplace assumptions about the capacity to manage or control the pandemic, but also to our equally commonplace assumptions about the nature of the world, the social, the economic, and the political—and *thereby* to the assumption that it is possible to posit the world as an object of knowing. (xviii)

If there is to be a pedagogy that can address the circuitous work of a social breakdown, the ego's capacity to destroy, and the interminable and fragile movement of reparation, then the symptoms of knowledge that come to be known as AIDS must become the subject of AIDS. This pedagogy might begin in the way Tony Kushner's (1984) play *Angels in American: Part Two: Perestroika* begins with a question without an answer. Says Alekssi Antedilluvianovich Prelapsarianov,

> The Great Question before us is: Are we doomed? The Great Question before us is: Will the Past release us? The Great Question before us is: Can we change? In Time? ... And *Theory*? How are we to proceed without *Theory*? (13)

Let us rethink these symptoms again with a methodological note given by Samuel Delany's (1988) short mediation on an event and its narrative reconstruction in his own education. Delany's method is to make an education from fiction because fiction has no authority and has the capacity to touch and be touched. This turn to literature serves as a model for pedagogy and social theory as literature has the capacity to imagine the fate of love and hate in learning (Young-Bruehl 1996).

We return to the ninth grade, where a teenage Delany (1988) has his first day in the prestigious Bronx High School of Science. Delany narrates this event in three tenses of time: the ethnographic, or the writing of detail; the reflective, or the consideration of significance and its anxieties; and the uncanny, or the force of secrets, where affect and idea touch in that erotic desire. The timing effects what Sue Golding (1993) calls, "a route a mapping, an impossible geography—impossible because *it exists and does not exist exactly at the same time*" (166).

The first telling is filled with the romance of the ethnographic. A 15-year-old Delany enters the classroom for that first day, peruses his new classmates, complies with the teacher's request that the students rearrange themselves through alphabetizing their seating order, and then he listens to the teacher's request that classmates nominate someone for the student government. A boy named Chuck nominates Delany, and Delany wins. In this ethnographic telling, perhaps too good to be true, everything happens well: his peers acclaim him, he meets a new friend, and his teacher seems friendly.

In the second telling, these details return as anxiety: "what strikes me is how quickly the written narrative closes out—puts it outside of language" (Delany 1988, 25). There is an older story the ethnographic present buries and preserves. What our 15-year-old Delany notices that first day and cannot bear to leave alone is the beautiful hand of Chuck. Delany begins to fall in love. In the second telling, there is the body of Chuck: his height, the color of his shirt, the fall of his hair, the tone of his skin, the shape of his hand, the way he sighs. In the momentary chaos of the students finding their seats, Delany loses sight of Chuck and, in this loss, feels the loneliness of that first day in a new school. And then there is panic: Had I only imagined Chuck? If I see him again will I see the same Chuck I first saw? Through the coincidence of alphabetical seating, Delany finds himself in a seat to the left of Chuck. And then their hands can finally touch. Their handshake leaves behind a trace. Yes it is the same Chuck who nominates Delany. And so the moves of anxiety momentarily rest in a community of daydreams, until the next troubling of the telling.

There is more to the story. That excess makes our third sense of time, the uncanny, open to what both wanted without notice. The uncanny can only be examined in bits and pieces for whereas its persistent force depends upon something returning that is no longer homey, its return is not complete. Delany maintains that his first ethnographic description does not explain his second try. He asks, "Why speak of what's uncomfortable to speak of?" (29). Delany might be worried about how his story can be understood, how his imagined readers may lend their own continuities, their own identificatory thinking, and then shatter his fragile yearnings. Delany may worry that the reader's capacity to undo what has already been done and to isolate affect from idea might wreck his reverie. He tests his narrative experiment with a paradox:

> If it is the split—the space between two columns (one resplendent and lucid with the writings of legitimacy, the other dark and hollow with the voices of the illegitimate)— that constitutes the subject, it is only after the Romantic inflation of the private into the subjective that such a split can even be located. (29–30)

That space that holds the split between falling in love and recounting that first day as if there were no fall isolates affect from ideation. The discomfort is the symptom of that split between rejection over love and an Eros that risks contact.

"Why speak of the uncomfortable?" Part of the answer, for Delany's (1988) method, is to locate 'the where' of discomfort and of course, the split:

> What damages might [this other story] do to women, children, the temperamentally more refined, the socially ignorant, the less well-educated, those with a barely controlled tendency toward the perverse . . . ? Since publishing it in most cases explains nothing or nothing of the public narrative, why not let it remain privy, personal, privileged—outside of language? (29)

Samuel Delany cannot keep outside of language what is inside himself. One boy falls in love with another boy. The authority says, 'Keep this love to yourself and therefore renounce it. Surrender your desires for the sake of the social. Identify with the aggressor. Undo, isolate, don't' touch.' We are back to not only the ethnographic story of AIDS in education but also the loss of love in education. It is a story that explains nothing, since it is designed not to notice. Delany's three temporalities gather the threads of love as an affective force. It must be so!

What then can be learned or better taken in? We will promise nothing and not expect too much. Ours is belated work that begins with the recognition that something can be destroyed, that education can inflict harm, strengthen superego prohibitions, turn these prohibitions into satisfaction, and isolate the ego from the id and the other. Because we are considering some psychical consequences of learning and unlearning, the three notions of time cannot be taken as progressions. Each turn opens variations of perspective, accidents, and coincidence.

In a pedagogy that attempts to address the question of AIDS, the first move resides in ethnographic stories. We can notice the contradictory details of the syndrome, of the HIV virus, of the woeful disregard of the events, of ACT UP, of the language of AIDS, of cultures and its discontented. The historicity of terminology must be accounted for, from the beginning around 1976 as a discourse of 'gay-related immune deficiency' to the four H-groups (Homosexuals, Hemophiliacs, Haitians, Heroin users) and on to what Paula Treichler (1988) has called, "the epidemic of signification." The ethnographic are stories of discourses and the constitution of bodies of knowledge mistaken as knowledge of bodies. But also this history should be situated in larger studies of illness and then of how societies across time go about distinguishing the healthy from the ill, the guilty from the innocent, the public from the risk group. The ethnographic stories must consider the cacophonous perspectives and arguments between and within communities. To defy the impulse to think that representation is the answer, the ethnographic can examine its own wounding: fiction, music, dance, film, journalism, the essay. The ethnographic move is curricular, necessary, and insufficient, demanding much in the way of engagement from teachers. As it turns, the ethnographic cannot avoid anxiety or the return of the repressed, the uncanny.

So the ethnography must be disrupted with a second move, a reflective narrative addressed to the ego's anxieties and defenses and to the strange time of delay. The significance has to do with the work of perception and reality testing. The ego will be warned that it is being interfered with, that it should try to notice when it stops noticing, that it should study its capacity to be touched and respond. This is an exploration of how the work of not noticing, although seemingly strengthening the ego's mechanisms of defense, only aggravates forces of aggression and militates against being touched. The pedagogy that must address the ego resides in the fault lines of resistance and notices where meaning breaks down, becomes fragile, loses its object, defies certitude, becomes ambivalent. There must be an address to the ego where it is asked to risk its history of love, enlarge itself for the other. The complex of symptoms that constitute the subject's responses to AIDS will be explored. We can bring in the specters of life once lived and consider the interminable work of mourning our losses.

In all of this, one more movement can be made. Open onto the uncanny, that place of secrets and, yes, love. Our topic then moves to safer sex practices, to the coming sexualities, and to the risk of love. This third move refuses the taboo against touching AIDS. And perhaps the ego can begin to place AIDS in its own everyday, in the ordinary process of thought. Still, as with any learning, a pedagogy that attempts to approach its own inconsolability, its own uncanny, is not in charge of itself. It takes its direction from life.

The pedagogy that offers no consolation, that cannot help education save itself, is the pedagogy that involves the destiny of love and the fragile work of making reparation because it once noticed its impulse to disregard, deny, and isolate. We must speak of the unspeakable but in so doing, we can also ask, What is making reparation in this learning?

Bibliography

Balint, Alice. 1954. *The Early Years of life: A Psychoanalytic Study*. New York: Basic Books.
Bollas, Christopher. 1992. *Becoming a Character: Psychoanalysis and Self Experience*. New York: Hill &Wang.
Britzman, Deborah P. 1998. *Lost Subjects, Contested Objects: Toward a Psychoanalytic Inquiry of Learning*. Albany, NY: State University of New York Press.
Canguilhem, Georges. 1991. *The Normal and the Pathological*. Translated by Carolyn R. Fawcett. New York: Zone Books.
Cornell, Drucilla. 1995. *The Imaginary Domain: Abortion, Pornography and Sexual Harassment*. New York: Routledge.
Delany, Samuel R. 1988. *The Motion of Light in Water: Sex and Science Fiction in the East Village, 1957–1965*. Middletown, CT: Wesleyan University Press.
———. 1994. "The Tale of Plagues and Carnivals, or: Some Informal Remarks toward the Modular Calculus, Part Five." In *Flight from Nevèrÿon*, 181–360. Middletown, CT: Wesleyan University Press.
Erikson, Erik H. 1968. *Identity: Youth and Crisis*. New York: W. W. Norton.

Felman, Shoshana. 1987. *Jacques Lacan and the Adventure of Insight: Psychoanalysis in Contemporary Culture*. Cambridge, MA: Harvard University Press.

Freud, Anna. (1936) 1995. *The Ego and the Mechanisms of Defense, Revised Edition. The Writings of Anna Freud, Vol. 2, 1936*. Madison, CT: International Universities Press.

Freud, Sigmund. 1953–1974. *The Standard Edition of the Complete Psychological Works of Sigmund Freud*, edited and translated by James Strachey, in collaboration with Anna Freud. 24 vols. London: Hogarth Press and Institute for Psychoanalysis.

———. 1923. "The Ego and the Id." In *The Standard Edition of the Complete Psychological Works of Sigmund Freud*, edited and translated by James Strachey, in collaboration with Anna Freud, vol. 19, 3–66. London: Hogarth Press and Institute for Psychoanalysis.

———. (1924) 1925. "An Autobiographical Study." In *The Standard Edition of the Complete Psychological Works of Sigmund Freud*, edited and translated by James Strachey, in collaboration with Anna Freud, vol. 20, 7–76. London: Hogarth Press and Institute for Psychoanalysis.

———. 1926a. "Inhibitions, Symptoms, and Anxieties." In *The Standard Edition of the Complete Psychological Works of Sigmund Freud*, edited and translated by James Strachey, in collaboration with Anna Freud, vol. 20, 87–174. London: Hogarth Press and Institute for Psychoanalysis.

———. 1926b. "The Question of Lay Analysis: Conversation with an Impartial Person." In *The Standard Edition of the Complete Psychological Works of Sigmund Freud*, edited and translated by James Strachey, in collaboration with Anna Freud, vol. 20, 179–258. London: Hogarth Press and Institute for Psychoanalysis.

———. (1932) 1933. "New Introductory Lectures on Psycho-analysis." In *The Standard Edition of the Complete Psychological Works of Sigmund Freud*, edited and translated by James Strachey, in collaboration with Anna Freud, vol. 22, 3–184. London: Hogarth Press and Institute for Psychoanalysis.

Golding, Sue. 1993. "Sexual Manners." *Public*, 8 (1): 161–68.

Haver, William Wendell. 1996. *The Body of this Death: Historicity and Sociality in the Time of AIDS*. Stanford, CA: Stanford University Press.

Klein, Melanie. (1937) 1975. "Love, Guilt and Reparation". In *Love, Guilt and Reparation and Other Works, 1921–1945*. Pp. 306-243. London: Hogarth Press.

Kushner, Tony. 1994. *Angles in America: A Gay Fantasia on National Themes, Part Two: Perestroika*. New York: Theatre Communications.

Lyotard, Jean-François. 1991. *The Inhuman: Reflections on Time*. Translated by Geoffrey Bennington and Rachel Bowlby. Stanford, CA: Stanford University Press.

Patton, Cindy. 1996. *Fatal Advice: How Safe-Sex Education Went Wrong*. Durham, NC: Duke University Press.

Readings, Bill. 1996. *The University in Ruins*. Cambridge MA: Harvard University Press.

Rose, Jacqueline. 1993. *Why War?: Psychoanalysis, Power, and the Return to Melanie Klein*. London: Blackwell.

Sachs, Hanns. 1947. "Community of Daydreams." In *Yearbook of Psychoanalysis Vol. I, 1945*, edited by Sandor Lorand, 281–302. New York: International Universities Press.

Schulman, Sarah. 1990. *People in Trouble*. New York: Dutton.

Silin, Jonathan G. 1995. *Sex, Death and the Education of Children: Our Passion for Ignorance in the Age of AIDS*. New York: Teachers College Press.

Treichler, Paula. (1988). AIDS, Homophobia, and Biomedical Discourse: An Epidemic of Signification. In *AIDS: Cultural Analysis, Cultural Activism*, edited by Douglas Crimp, 31–70. Cambridge, MA: MIT Press.

Winnicott, Donald W. 1986. *Home Is Where We Start From: Essays by a Psychoanalyst*. New York: W. W. Norton.

Young-Bruehl, Elisabeth. 1996. *The Anatomy of Prejudices*. Cambridge, MA: Harvard University Press.

Endnotes

1 The argument Rose (1993) makes for an ethics of failure emerges from her mediation on the question, why war? Rose considers war as the limit of absolute knowledge, a time when cause and effect collapse and when projection and reality cannot be separated. If war signifies the failure of knowledge, the violent attempt to reunify knowledge through war only makes the matter worse. Rose concludes her essay: "Knowledge will be possible, only if we are willing to suspend the final purpose and ends of knowledge in advance" (37). Her view works against the enterprise of education and its founding insistence on the linear relation between teaching and learning.

2 Georges Canguilhem's (1991) discussion of the concepts of illness and health makes this same point:

> The problem of the existence of perfect health is analogous. As if perfect health were not a normative concept. . . . Strictly speaking a norm does not exist, it plays its role, which is to devalue existence by allowing its correction. To say that perfect health does not exist is simply saying that the concept of health is not one of an existence, but of a norm whose function and value is to be brought into contact with existence in order to stimulate modification. (77)

3 Erikson's (1968) notion of a communality of egos reminds educators of the complex circulation of influence and resistance in the classroom. But it is also a way to consider Freud's insistence that social processes and psychical processes are indistinguishable. Hanns Sachs (1947) is also concerned with influence but the influence of literature on psychical freedom. Thus, a community of daydreams is not a community made from identity but from reverie and the capacity to imagine the poetic creations of the unconscious. This leads Sachs to advocate for the work of the daydream to come closer to the work of art, to renounce the wish for heroism and rescue, and live without ulterior motives in order to meet the unconscious. The Sachs sentence could read "Where id was there art shall become."

4 The pathetic history of condom distribution in schools and clean needle distribution campaigns in clinics in North American are key examples of what Cindy Patton (1996) has called "the national pedagogy". In the decade of the 1980s, one can also bring into discussion Jessie Helms's social policy of refusing funding for safer-sex campaigns that address gay and lesbian subjects.

5 In a short section titled "Never Mind," Bollas (1992) situates the violence of innocence as the refusal of relationality: "Clearly it is a form of denial, but one in which we observe not the subject's denial of external perception, but the subject's denial of the other's perception" (180). Two relations are being denied: the self's otherness and the other's otherness.

6 Resistance is one of the most difficult concepts in psychoanalysis because the term implicates thinking as one of its primary methods. The problem is not that a better idea can somehow transcend psychical wounds. This is why Lyotard (1991) argues that thinking is a form of suffering.

7 Bill Reading's (1996) study of the university raises the stakes of an inconsolable pedagogy and the need for a social bond to be rethought without alibis such as grand narratives of emancipation or melancholy longings for a lost wholeness: "The sheer fact of obligation to others is something that exceeds subjective consciousness, which is why we never get free of our obligations to others, which is why nobody is a model citizen (the citizen who would not have any bond to anyone else in the community because he or she would stand for the community as a whole)" (186).

8 For discussion on the failure of the calculations of knowledge in the pandemic, see Samuel Delany's (1994) novella "The Tale of Plagues and Carnivals," or "Some Informal Remarks toward the Modular Calculus, Part Five." The novella was published three times, and each succeeding edition carried a new appendix and postscript. The first postscript summarized its own symptomology: "The Tale of Plagues and Carnivals," is, of course, a work of imagination; and to the extent it is a document, largely what it documents is misinformation, rumour, and wholly untested guesses at play through a limited social section of New York City during 1982 and 1983, mostly before the 23 April 1984 announcement of the discovery of a virus ... as the overwhelmingly probably case of AIDS" (361). The novella, then, becomes not just an ethical mediation on an ethical problem, of whether the reader distinguishes between the study and the stories of misprision. The unit of analysis, if such a reduction can be made, in constituting this AIDS novella, is the self/other relation, followed as the course of an event and its alteration by otherness.

CHAPTER 6

The Death of Curriculum?

How strange to confront curriculum and all that it holds as a burial place, a crypt. But how very difficult it must be to see in knowledge the death of the object and to ponder from this death how life might be lived. For Shakespeare—and he, too, is caught in such a crypt—encountering the work of living means confronting the confusions of some cruel negations: to praise and not to bury; to be or not to be? As for curriculum, how does one bury and not praise its objectives? And, if we could somehow sort through all the objects the curriculum leaves behind, how would we decide which were worthy and which were useless? Even more, can we imagine the lost curriculum? How does one come to mourn the losses that go under the name curriculum? Can we decide not to preserve a moribund curriculum and instead ask, Why curriculum at all?

The questions I offer suppose a certain labor of thought, what Freud (1917) called "the work of mourning." In using the term *work*, Freud does not give us a sense of the duration of grief or ways to devise its stages. This work of mourning cannot be prescribed. Freud was interested in the interminable effort the mourner must expend—what he called 'decathexis'—to let go and work through loss as the work of mourning. Essentially, the work of mourning is a work of resignification of daily meanings and libidinal attachments. The mourner herself must change and be willing to be affected—touched—by memory, by that which is gone but still exerts a force of loss into our present. How something comes to matter and why things matter when they are no longer present are part of what the work of mourning gives us to consider. Because the problem of meaning is tied to how to signify its loss, the work of mourning is also subject to melancholia.

I want to consider what the work of mourning offers to this labor of curriculum and then raise some rather essential questions: What is the relation between loss and knowledge in the curriculum and what interrupts the work of mourning? Rather than assert a specific content or argue for the introduction of ignored voices that can somehow avoid this work of mourning, I will be suggesting a constitutive problem with knowledge itself. Some philosophers, when speaking of knowledge, have called this interruption, *peripeteia*: a fall, an unexpected reversal of circumstance. The problem of loss is genetic to the very structure of knowledge. To notice that the inadvertent curriculum is subject to such sudden reversals, to accidental stumbling, to turning against itself, and to becoming affected by the events made from its own fall, to notice these emotional situations may well be the difficult stakes that allow us to ask, 'Why curriculum?' When and how do we notice the curriculum that cannot be in charge of itself, the curriculum without mastery?

To ponder such events, I turn to Freud's thoughts on war, death, and the work of mourning. Other ghosts who haunt the curriculum, not so much by their presence but by their absence, will also be called upon to comment such as Melanie Klein, Robert Musil, and Wilfred Bion. They are brought into discussion to notice something that the moribund curriculum foreclosed, namely, the problem of what it is to work through woeful disregard, envy, and the loss of love. While none of them asked the question— Why curriculum?—they did notice something difficult about knowledge and thinking that will be put to use.

Let us be affected by what the author Robert Musil (1993, 49) named "ill-tempered observations," a preliminary labor of discomfort. One of his essays under this banner is titled "Surrounded by Poets and Thinkers." This might be a metaphor for curriculum unless, of course, the curriculum empties itself of such creatures in the name of skill development and, yes, even competency and readiness. Then we would only be surrounded by all that we lack. Still, Musil was not one to idealize culture; after all, he was also the author of a two-volume unfinished novel, *The Man Without Qualities*, his meditation on the *fin- de- siècle* and its collapse from the weight of its own anxiety (Musil 1995). Even if poets and thinkers surrounded the curriculum, for someone like Musil this crowd would only heighten anxiety. Here is his ill-tempered warning: Being surrounded can feel claustrophobic or even too competitive. Musil as journalist (1993) noted that before World War II, Germany had more than 1,000 magazines and 30,000 books published each year. Although at one time this may have offered new sorts of publics, by 1933, huge public burnings of books, including those authored by Sigmund Freud, also took place. How can we think of the coexistence of such events? Musil thought of such mass production as something other than a culture's capacity for intellectual achievement, calling such frenzy, "the spread of a dangerous group-mania. Infected by this mania, thousands of little groups each peddle their own set notion of life, so that it ought not to surprise us if soon a genuine paranoiac will hardly still be able to resist competing with the amateurs" (1993, 76). So, too, in our own times: a thousand tiny curricula vie for attention; some try to cure a thousand tiny learning disabilities while others take away a thousand ideas and a thousand tiny ambivalences we make from knowledge. No doubt there is confusion as to where to turn, yet suppose the confusion at stake is not the problem of which curriculum to deliver but rather, and once again, why curriculum at all?

Before Musil, another Viennese citizen noticed something of the confusion of his own times and asked what is it to think from within confusion:

> In the confusion of our time in which we are caught up, relying as we must on one-sided information, standing too close to the great changes that have already taken place or are beginning to, and without a glimmering of the feature that is being shaped, we ourselves are at a loss as to the significance of the impressions which press in upon us and as to the value of the judgments which we form. (Freud 1915, 275)

So begins Freud's (1915) terse essay "Thoughts for the Times on War and Death," written at the beginning of World War I. Freud questions the proximity and limits of what we might make from knowledge but cannot answer the haunting question the child always asks: "Why war?" Knowledge cannot come to the rescue because war, Freud goes on to suggest, is the absolute breakdown of meaning, the most aggressive, repetitive, and evil return of a sociality's refusal to learn from the failure of knowledge. Can we consider the curriculum in such ill-tempered terms and ask, 'Why curriculum?' Freud can only write of his own disillusionment toward the capacity of knowledge to put itself in the service of life. And then he offers a long string of attendant losses when knowledge no longer matters: enjoyment; the capacity to judge; the interest in creating and sustaining affective ties with strangers; indeed, the loss of any distinction between the human's susceptibility to culture and its other susceptibility to what can happen when the forces of instinctual satisfaction meet the drive to destruction. The very capacity to think, to take one's own time, is dissociated and confused with perhaps what Musil saw as dangerous group mania and what Freud would come to see as melancholia. We become susceptible, give ourselves over to confusion in the hope that at least we will have something left. In times of war and death and in the confusion of time such epistemological and ontological chaos invokes, there may also follow a felt betrayal as to what has happened to all that is idealized as the best in humanity. Freud sees this betrayal as beside the point. His view is bleaker: "In reality our fellow-citizens have not sunk so low as we feared, because they had never risen so high as we believed" (1915, 286). Can we bring such a view to our own faith in knowledge and dare to say that the curriculum cannot sink so low because it has never risen so high?

But what is the nature of the confusion at stake? Can we think of the defense of confusion without resorting to the call for more clarity, easier language, simpler ideas, better skills, less convolution? Such an orientation to clearing up confusion leads to a rather stringent curriculum that mistakes knowledge for answers and that collapses the symbol with that which it represents. The sort of confusion Freud had in mind was more difficult, a state of mental vulnerability in which the problem was how to distinguish thinking from ignorance, absence from presence, and love from hate. Consider the care Melanie Klein gives to confusion. In "Envy and Gratitude," Klein ([1957]1975) outlines some inaugurating states of mental confusions: the confusion of good and bad, the confusion of persecution and guilt, the confusion of the internal world with the external world, the confusion of self and object, and the confusion of learning and mastery. "Such confusion," writes Klein, "interferes with the recognition of psychic reality, which contributes to the understanding and realistic perception of external reality" (221). But Klein also reminds us that this sort of confusion is also a psychic achievement: without these dilemmas, an individual would be unable to think or even recognize the terrors and pleasures of symbolization. The recognition of psychical reality—as other to ordinary reality and the classroom clock—may accompany confusion, provided that confusion is considered worthy as a struggle with having to mean. While Klein reminds us of that other war, the war within that inaugurates psychical reality, Freud (1915) suggests something of how the world at war also forecloses the capacity to think.

There is, then, a twofold paradox offered in Freud's (1915) essay, a problem that offers something more difficult to the interminable question, 'Why curriculum?' If war is a time when we cannot think beyond the reach of confusion, when the difference between reality and fantasy dissolves—so that we cannot finally know if we made our enemies, if we need our enemies, or if we have actual enemies—if such melancholia predominates, how is it possible to have any thoughts on war and death? And then, what does war and death have to do with peace and life? Freud begins his thoughts with a prior moment: we can only think when the object is lost, and this absence moves thinking closer to the work of mourning. If such is the case, can the claim of the death of curriculum invoke the work of mourning, the work of thinking the loss of our thoughts, and so the coming to terms with what has been lost?

Part of the work of mourning involves recognizing loss, not just what has been lost to the world but what has been lost in the self. Freud (1917) distinguishes mourning from melancholia although both involve a confusion of loss: "Mourning is regularly the reaction to the loss of a loved person, or to the loss of some abstraction which has taken the place of one, such as one's country, liberty, an ideal and so on" (243). Even the loss of an idea invokes mourning. But if the work of mourning is to be uninterrupted and not dissolve into melancholia, the mourner must be able to somehow acknowledge what is lost in both the world and the self and somehow try to find new ideas and people in the world. "In mourning it is the world which has become poor and empty; in melancholia it is the ego itself" (246). The melancholic curriculum impoverishes, confusing the difficulty of knowledge with the knowledge of difficulty.

The loss we confront in the field of curriculum is the loss of our capacity to recognize our own psychical reality as being out of joint with ordinary reality. By this I mean that when the field can only argue over which knowledge is proper, the question of why knowledge at all cannot be thought. Can we bear to consider the death of curriculum apropos to a time that returns itself back to an earlier state, a time of stasis, a curriculum subject to its own death drive? To be sure, there is something difficult in any attempt to think the death of curriculum for it forces us, albeit metaphorically, to confront the question of our present disillusionment with the promise of knowledge to return what has been lost. Many have noticed that this disillusionment toward knowledge persists as one of the 20th century's great epistemological themes and is acted out, albeit unconsciously, in the fields of curriculum (Britzman 1998). The illusion is supported by a series of defences the field of curriculum employs: the curriculum as technical, as government, as genealogy, as preparation, as measurement, as something that is capable of speaking for itself. Disillusionment resides somewhere between the poles of catastrophe and redemption, as a nation at risk, as crumbling standards, as moral vacuum, as recruitment device, as perversity. Whether this disillusionment takes the form of incredulity toward meta-narratives, as Lyotard (1987) suggests in his report on the status of knowledge in universities; whether, as Willinsky (1998) offers in his study of knowledge in the age of the internet, the disillusionment transforms into the politics of exasperation over the sheer amount of information that litters the metaphoric super information highway and turns us into consumers of non-events; whether one can notice, as Readings (1996) noticed, that calls for excellence in schools and universities have no referent; whether this disillusionment is acted out in the confines of censorship, in the disassembling of bilingual education, in the refusal of sex education and homoerotic images, or the wiring of schools for surveillance, and in the very capacity to think, the anxiety, as Haver (1996, 23) has put it, is made from our own limits: "Not even education can save us as now."

All these forms of incredulity may actually repeat a more archaic disillusionment: our attitude toward death. What does curriculum have to do with our attitude toward death if the curriculum itself offers tribute to its own burial? If the central dynamic of curriculum is closer to the compulsion to repeat its own incapacity to notice what goes on in its name, if the curriculum interrupts, through its technology, its methods, its structure, its pedagogy, our capacity to mourn, to notice loss, how then can we who are the creators of curriculum ask, "Why curriculum?"

Freud (1915) suggests in his "Thoughts" essay something quite difficult about thinking itself, that if the urge to think is viewed as the means for exceeding the body, considered as an experience of sheer will, as treated like an escape from the interminable problem of perception and reality, and as functioning "reliably only when it is removed from the influences of strong emotional impulses" (287), then that which disillusions thought cannot be thought. Affect is the constitutive limit of thought, or what Certeau (1988) much later will argue as, that which wounds the illusion of composed knowledge. If knowledge cannot compose itself, and if its strategies of distinction and upkeep are so fragile in its susceptibility to the affects of distress, denial, disavowal, and so on, then what will be the future of knowledge, indeed, the future of our capacity to think for the fields of curriculum?

These questions are different from the death-of-the-subject claims so common in philosophical disputes. For even there, the text could live beyond the author, thought could be abstracted, and so there was something beyond death that could trouble life. The claim being examined here is not the melancholic one of berating the love that is lost, the object that is gone, although certain nostalgic views of restoring the curriculum as capable of managing its subjects so that no one will ever get lost seem, to me, as a symptom of melancholic loss. If thought must lose itself to begin to think itself, if confusion can inaugurate something more, if the finding of the lost object is always a re-finding, then what is this work but a speculation that poses the work of mourning as the obligation of learning to live with death?

"But this attitude of ours toward death," Freud goes on to write in the second section of this haunted essay, "has a powerful effect on our lives" (1915, 290). One part of this attitude, particularly in times of peace, is incredulity toward death, where death is not considered a necessity of life but as a chance event that happens to others. In times of war, our attitudes toward death alter but not so much, Freud insists, that one can find a new attitude. For Freud, something within resists knowledge of our own death, and this resistance is put into service of exasperation toward death. The conflict, then, is between acknowledging the loss that is death and denying the possibility that each of us will experience the utter singularity of our own death. However, even this view is unsatisfactory to Freud. He goes on to make a rather startling point: the beginning of our capacity to speculate does not emerge from an intellectual problem of confronting pictures of death and thereby reflecting on death; speculation, or the capacity to think, begins from the conflict of ambivalence, made when one confronts one's feelings for the death of another. The "spirit of inquiry" (293) begins with the capacity to think about the split between thoughts and feelings, between love and hate. "Death," writes Jacqueline Rose (1993), "is a problem, but not because we cannot surmount its loss or imagine our own death, but because it forces us to acknowledge that what belongs to us most intimately is also a stranger or an enemy . . . [so that] thought provoked by mourning takes the form of dissociation" (19). Inquiry, in this view, is a borderline concept, a confusion of traumatic experience made from being torn within how to think about loss, about our own capacity to destroy, and about our own alienness. Paradoxically, thinking begins in dissociation, a dissociation that renders indistinct the wounds of affect and that which resists thought.

Our own constitutional ambivalence, however, seems to be acted out as opposed to worked through in the very epistemology of curriculum. Ambivalence, of loving and hating the same object, is just the beginning of the problem of passionate attachment. But more often than not, the field of curriculum seeks to strip our relation to knowledge of any form of ambivalence and in doing so finds it inconceivable that feelings toward knowledge cannot sustain the illusion of certainty. Indeed, uncertainty, feeling torn as to what to believe, being in a state of confusion, and acting as if these experiences are somehow a problem only curriculum can solve, preserves the moribund curriculum and a melancholy education. We can ask: What does the curriculum bury in order to preserve itself? When Freud ([1929] 1930) glanced at the school curriculum he noticed civilization and discontentment and its violent origins: "Even to-day, the history of the world which our children learn at school is essentially a series of murders of people" (292). If the act of civilization requires a violent origin, curriculum seems to be the unconscious burial ground where the repetition of the society's violent origins persists. Can contemporary students and teachers understand these events with, as Freud put it, "the conflict of feeling at the death of loved yet alien and hated persons" (293)? What happens when we can admit ambivalence toward both defeat and victory? What can actually be learned from studying or recounting the violent origins of a nation, a social, and an institution, if we have difficulty believing in our own our otherness—death—and if the alienness of others cannot be viewed as a symptom of our own alienness?

Freud does not offer any answers for the questions he raised about thought in times of war and death. He does suggest that making life tolerable is the first obligation of living, and illusions that promise a life without conflict can only make it harder to live. The last sentence of his essay suggests the angst raised when death is moved to the center of life: "*Si vis vitam, para mortem*. If you want to endure life, prepare yourself for death" (1915, 300). If war strips away this paradox, presenting to the living the horror of their own mortality but not the tragedy of the other, the aggression that war requires allows one to forget that preparation and renders intolerable what Jacqueline Rose (1993) names as "the ethics of failure" (36), or a way of thinking in difficult times. War, Rose argues, represents the limit of absolute knowledge even as the reasons for war seem to sustain a view of knowledge as capable of answering the question, 'Why war?' So, too, with the violent origins of curriculum. Knowledge is lost and found somewhere between the outside war and the war within. It is subject to both flaws, but not in ways that can be predicted, controlled, or even mastered. But if knowledge, indeed, if the knowledge we call curriculum is to speak to something alien in us, if it can tolerate this reversal, this peripeteia, it will have to begin with suspending its own ends, acknowledging what has been lost in the name of curriculum with an 'ethics of failure' that might invoke a certain work of thinking, Freud called the work of mourning.

Finally, one must admit a strange paradox to these sorts of thoughts on the death of the curriculum, for part of the dilemma is that experience, yes, even teaching experience, is irrelevant. These thoughts on the death of the curriculum offer nothing to the question of what shall we do on Monday; surely our means of resuscitating what goes on under the name of the practical should by now be exhausted. Mondays arrive whether we are prepared or not. But also our preparation will always be insufficient because the curriculum cannot predict the intimate felt relations of knowledge at stake in learning. That is to say, Monday's curriculum cannot settle the confusion of our times. More urgently, the very posing of this Monday problem may well defend against the deeper anxiety that Musil (1993) noticed: How do we spend the time that we have? How do we learn to live? The problem for any day is this: what is it to think with others in education? Part of our work may be to encounter the confusion of our times, not in the ways that Musil or Freud warned us against but perhaps closer to what Melanie Klein thought of as the working through of confusion, as an interest in recognizing psychical reality and defenses against the emotional world. Part of the recognition would be ill tempered. What would have to be acknowledged is the idea that we are affected by that which exceeds consciousness, intention, and will. We are affected by what we do not know. Another part of the recognition might be loving, that there is something tender about fragility, dependency and vulnerability.

Bion (1977) gives us a sense of this paradox:

> If a thought without a thinker comes along, it may be what is a 'stray thought', or it could be a thought with the owner's name and address upon it, or it could be a 'wild thought.' Of course, if it is wild, you might try to domesticate it. . . .What I am concerned with at the moment is the wild thoughts that turn up and for which there is no possibility of being able to trace immediately any kind of ownership or even any sort of way of being aware of the genealogy of that particular thought. (27)

It seems to me that if the curriculum is to offer us anything like the experience of having to think, then the lost and probably wild question—why curriculum?—must be found.

Bibliography

Bion, Wilfred. R. 1997. *Taming Wild Thoughts*. Edited by Francesca Bion. London: Karnac Books.

Britzman, Deborah P. 1998. *Lost Subjects, Contested Objects: Toward a Psychoanalytic Inquiry of Learning*. Albany: State University of New York Press.

Certeau, Michel de. 1988. *The Writing of History*. Translated by Tom Conley. New York: Columbia University Press.

Freud, Sigmund. 1953–1974. *The Standard Edition of the Complete Psychological Works of Sigmund Freud*, edited and translated by James Strachey, in collaboration with Anna Freud. 24 vols. London: Hogarth Press and Institute for Psychoanalysis.

———. 1915. "Thoughts for the Times on War and Death." In *The Standard Edition of the Complete Psychological Works of Sigmund Freud*, edited and translated by James Strachey, in collaboration with Anna Freud, vol. 14, 273–301. London: Hogarth Press and Institute for Psychoanalysis.

———. 1917. "Mourning and Melancholia." In *The Standard Edition of the Complete Psychological Works of Sigmund Freud*, edited and translated by James Strachey, in collaboration with Anna Freud, vol. 14, 239–58. London: Hogarth Press and Institute for Psychoanalysis.

———. (1929) 1930. *Civilization and Its Discontents*. In *The Standard Edition of the Complete Psychological Works of Sigmund Freud*, edited and translated by James Strachey, in collaboration with Anna Freud, vol. 21, 59–145. London: Hogarth Press and Institute for Psychoanalysis.

Haver, William. 1996. *The Body of This Death: Historicity and Sociality in the Time of AIDS*. Palo Alto, CA: Stanford University Press.

Klein, Melanie. (1957)1975. "Envy and Gratitude." In *Envy and Gratitude and Other Works 1946-1963*. Pp. 176-235. London: Hogarth Press.

Lyotard, Jean-Francois. 1987. *The Postmodern Condition: A Report on Knowledge*. Translated by Geoff Bennington and Brian Massumi. Manchester, UK: Manchester University Press.

Musil, Robert. 1993. *Posthumous Papers of a Living Author*. Translated by Peter Wortsman. New York: Penguin.

———. 1995. *The Man without Qualities, Vol. I and II*. Translated by Sophie Wilkins. New York: Alfred Knopf.

Readings, Bill. 1996. *The University in Ruins*. Cambridge, MA: Harvard University Press.

Rose, Jacqueline. 1993. *Why War?—Psychoanalysis, Politics, and the Return to Melanie Klein*. Oxford, UK: Blackwell.

Willinsky, John. 1998. "Automata Data and the Future of Knowledge." Presentation at the American Educational Research Association Annual Conference, San Diego, California, April 13–17.

CHAPTER 7

The Fate of Being a Stranger

WITHOUT AT FIRST knowing why, one comes across a phrase that provokes thinking, crystallizes affect, and lends an odd integrity to, and even helps contain, disparate preoccupations and an aimlessness that also make up the mind. Even more, a phrase can fall like a shadow on narrative and urge thinking along the rough edges of meaning. And this happened for me with Julia Kristeva's (1991) haunting meditation on the fate of being a stranger used to think within our contemporary preoccupations with war, ethnic hatred, globalization, the crumbling of civil and human rights, the burdens of unresolved history, the hatred of the immigrant, and even the right to revolt. Such fate becomes a way for thinking of education in its most speculative time and not as outcome, prediction, or management but as learning to live with the course of one's life. What is it to listen to the stranger who also narrates the terrible feel of social breakdown within her attempts at reparation, atonement, love, and friendship?

Much of Kristeva's writing is dedicated to the stranger. Kristeva's (1991) *Strangers to Ourselves* meditates on how the position of the stranger also makes a notion of 'us.' She asked about the relation between acknowledging and so recognizing "the time in which understanding and affinity founder" (1). And let us note this very provocative, peripatetic, and untimely phrasing made from the breakdown of meaning. This fate can solely belong to a subject, that is, to a person who is literally a stranger; it can reach as well into an internal condition, where one is stranger from within; this fate can lend difference to the problem of otherness, and feelings of alienation. With this foundering of affinity, there remains the quest for an ethical encounter. When do I encounter the stranger? How does the stranger encounter new geographies? And what becomes of the stranger in me? We would do well to think whether education has anything to say. This fate of being a stranger begins with an accident of birth, of having to be born and then needing to be greeted by those already here. That fate of being a stranger is intimately tied to what Hannah Arendt (1993) calls beginnings: "The essence of education is natality, the fact that human beings are *born* into the world" (174). Here then is a promise for the new, a potential self, and for those already here, an obligation. And this fate of being a stranger can be animated by personal action, such as when one just walks or runs away from the familiar. If this fate is not yet an experiment in thought, narrative renders it so.

Kristeva (2001) suggested that uncertain fate when she termed the 20th century "Our Psychoanalytic Century," a century of information, education, and testimony. After all, with psychoanalysis there can be introduced a new relation to madness: listening to it, describing it, and freely associating with it in its language. Often called 'the talking cure,' psychoanalysis took language to its farthest outpost and permitted words to signify without borders. One can think of the surrealist movement's work of taking language apart and reassembling it in ways that made the ordinary feel utterly estranged and fractured. Everyday language suffers this fate. Psychoanalysts encounter language as if it were a stranger. Meaning must pass through dreams, phantasy, psychical reality, the grammar of affect, and the other's interpretation.

Some of the thinkers I have been keeping company with ushered in the 20th century, while others bid it farewell. They all testified to the century's devastations, its breakdowns of meanings, its internal and external catastrophes, its traumatic repetitions, and even what Adorno ([1959] 2002) in his lectures on Kant, would call the Kantian Block: "it is a kind of metaphysical mourning, a kind of memory of what is best, of something we must not forget, but that we are never the less compelled to forget" (176). There is something unbridgeable between the outside world and our understanding of it. We can think about our limits but cannot be without them. And the thinkers discussed here knew this, even as they also held a faith in our capacity to think deeply, not as instrumental rationality, or as in Hegel's 'evil genius,' but rather they all treated thinking as a means to construct a certain freedom from an uncertain fate. They thought through the structures of the biography, the travelogue, the novel, the short story, and the correspondence. Many occupied the same difficult years, from around 1926 through 1939. The extremity of difficulty however belongs to us. We only know this now although how to use this knowledge worried them all. Their search for meaning leaves us with difficult questions. What sense are we to make of our own time, now reduced to a calendar date, an emergency number, a prohibition against interpretation, September 11 notwithstanding? What is it to think of strangers here and there in these untimely times?

With her meditation on the fate of being a stranger, Kristeva may have also been thinking of Hannah Arendt. This philosopher became a stranger in her own country, escaped Germany and, in exile, settled by 1941 in New York City with other exiles from the Frankfort school. A study of Arendt's world was the first of Kristeva's three-volume trilogy experiments with the fate of narrative revolts. Her trilogy's subtitle tells the whole story in miniature *Female Genius: Life, Madness, Words—Hannah Arendt* (2001a), *Melanie Klein* (2001b), and *Colette* (2004). There would be the philosopher, the psychoanalyst, and the poet, a trilogy of thinking about thinking. Kristeva had the audacity to take an old yet still startling question—Can a woman be a genius?—and wrench it within narrative revolt. Her use of the word *genius* was, in itself, ingenious. Kristeva is after a way of representing the qualities of originality in thinking, what she (2002) would also call "the intimacy of revolt." Its material is made from the ordinary— the flora and fauna of the silent, the forgotten, the discarded, and the ignored—and also from the delirium of history, indeed, from life, madness, and words. And the architecture of this trilogy brings into relief the life work of their education. To set up education in this bold way is to open it to revolt, to surpassing inhibition, convention, and, yes, even community. These women figures perform a learning to live after the experience of education. This education, then, is formation, resistance, limitation, and affinity.

When Kristeva (2001b) offered that haunting phrase, "the fate of being a stranger," (194) she was speaking specifically about the psychoanalyst Melanie Klein and wondering how Klein's leaving of Budapest for Berlin and then finally to settle in London by 1926 shadowed her interest in thinking with the strangeness of a psychical reality called "phantasy." Klein was a stranger to English, and although she wrote her most important works in this language, she passed through Hungarian, German, French, and baby talk. She was, simply put, a stranger to many countries, but the country that mattered most, was the psychic reality of the other. Was this the fate that prepared Klein for the difficulties her theory would bring to psychoanalysis and what she claimed for the infant? Was Klein more willing to cross the line into "Our Psychoanalytic Century" and so move as close to madness as she could? Kristeva writes of Klein as a woman genius, by which she meant that Klein was both original and courageous in her theory of knowledge and in what she claimed could urge and destroy our capacity to think. And if it is Klein's fate to be tied to unconscious anxiety, to have introduced us all to some of our own crowded and terrified internal world, it is through her notion of the urge for reparation and gratitude that opens this world to welcome the stranger within and without.

"In the early 1920s, as a young journalist in Vienna and then in Berlin," writes Michel Hoffman in his excellent introduction to the novelist Joseph Roth's (1894–1939) journalist work, "Roth wrote numerous articles drawing attention to the awful plight of refugees and displaced persons, Jews and others– in the aftermath of World War One, The Russian Revolution, and the redrawing of [European] national boundaries" (Roth 2001, xiii–xiv). Roth's (2001) *Wandering Jews* documents what came to be known as 'the Jewish problem,' the fate of becoming strangers in one's own country. The novelist Roth also gives this travelogue a terrible twist in how he addresses his readership, in the ways he arranges different communities in snapshots that catch what is least expected and intended, and in how his sparse sentences perform an ironic glance. Roth wrote of rivalry between Jewish communities: cultural breakdowns between the Jewish ghettos in the East and the assimilated Jewry of the West. These geographies were strange to each other, and Roth's is a reflection on how a people split and divide themselves and how they are divided and disparaged by larger worlds no matter where they are. Each kaleidoscopic turn brings more ironies to bear on displacement as Roth comments on the daily lives of Jews, city by city, dream by dream, and street by street.

Originally, Roth's sketches were completed and published in 1926. Its last chapter is a rather exuberant and premature celebration of Jews in the Soviet Union. Isaac Babel would make this same mistake: he, too, was a stranger who wrote of strangers he knew. There were Jewish gangsters, intellectuals with glasses who want to ride with the Cossacks, disappointed writers, and communities no longer here. So, there was also this twist of fate. The company Babel kept was suspended between the desire to belong and the fate of the stranger. Like Roth, Babel, too, was a journalist of sorts, writing reports from Petersburg (1918), from Georgia (1922–24), and then France (1935). There were also haunting short stories and always the prose: sparse, sketchy, maybe even nervous.

Babel was arrested in 1939 during one of Stalin's great purges. He was not heard of again. But over the course of many years, his books, diaries, and short stories were translated from Russian into English. As if to usher in the new century, his complete works were published in English (Babel 2002). That history crisscrossed the writer Joseph Roth.

By 1937, Roth adds a heartbreaking preface to a new edition of *Wandering Jews*, referring now to the rise and popularity of national socialism and its genocidal violence toward Jews. A devistating turn for education occurs in Roth's reflection: "When catastrophe occurs, people at hand are shocked into helplessness" (125). Roth observed we like our catastrophes to be brief, "[b]ut chronic catastrophes are so unpalatable to neighbors that they gradually become indifferent to them and their victims, if not downright impatient" (125). Contemporary readers may stumble upon Adorno's Kantian Block, noticing the tension between memory and forgetting yet being unable to avoid it. Readers may also be left with something of Roth's bitterness and irony as he reflects on his own sense of helplessness: "I wish I had the grace to suggest some way out of our present difficulties. But honesty, one of the often-unsung muses of the writer, forces me to bring this second foreword of mine to a pessimistic conclusion" (125). Here then is the trauma of being a stranger.

A different fate is played out in the very long correspondence between the Hungarian analyst Sándor Ferenczi (1873–1933) and Sigmund Freud (1856–1939) of Vienna (Brabant et al., 1992; 1996; 2000). Three volumes of their letters are now translated into English; they span the years 1908 to 1933 and end the year of Ferenczi's death. The correspondence takes us to personal places: of the founding arguments of psychoanalysis, of disappointed but at times exuberant friendships, of loyalties made and betrayed, of summer vacations and travel, of civil wars in Europe and family deaths, of economic despair, of psychoanalytic misadventures, and of the lateness of learning from psychical life. These letters previewed new psychoanalytic words and hint at the drama behind the publications. They now lend insight into the strange trajectory of Freud's and Ferenczi's work. Letters reported on the ordinary and extraordinary, on the world of spirits and that other world of dreams and its interpretation. And they also tell a story of the asymmetry of friendship: the problem of boundaries between friends, of different affective investments, of disappointed hopes. As these two analysts narrated the fissures of friendship through admitting their voluntary and involuntary differences, both were developing a position for analysts. For Freud it was neutrality and abstinence; Ferenczi desired 'mutual analysis,' intimacy, even a kiss.

In letters they tried to work through their differences, and that set the terms of their correspondence: Ferenczi was an exuberant 25-year-old, just beginning to learn about the new psychoanalysis when he first wrote to a 52-year-old Freud. Freud reluctantly agreed to serve as Ferenczi's analyst, although World War I stopped this short. And this inequality, along with startling mishaps, fueled their respective personal fates: for Ferenczi, it was the fate of feeling misunderstood and unloved; for Freud, it was the fate of becoming older, feeling the hastening of time as terribly strange.

If Freud and Ferenczi could not stop reporting to each another on their respective lives, on what they thought about, Sebald's (2001) strangely haunting dialogue that makes the novel *Austerlitz* takes us to the underside of narration, where one's own history is estranged and where recollection itself is buried. Here we also find features of Kristeva's architecture of 'life, madness, words.' *Austerlitz* brings readers into the new century by putting history back where it belongs, not as censorship, amnesia, or loyalty but as simply depth. How is it possible, the novel's protagonists seem to ask one another while the reader must overhear, to learn from absence and erasure? And how, the novel asks of the reader, does one move from repeating the traumatic perception of catastrophic history to mourning the loss of affinity, to conceive of history as that which is no longer here yet still pressures our lives? In this last novel of W. G. Sebald (1944–2001), readers enter indirectly the deceptions, accidents, and nervous conditions of history, identity, and sociality. There, the fate of being a stranger takes its time unfolding, slowly setting out long discarded and blurry details of history. They pile up to devastating effects: we are returned to the Shoah and World War II, not to relive it but to ponder what comes after, how, for instance, the idea of innocence, neutrality, and civility lost its protective glow and now used to deflect implication. Could our commemorative practices, the monuments we hope for, the ones we receive, be for education a second trauma?

Austerlitz is a man burdened with too much and too little history; he is not who he thought, and he slowly learns this, as he haltingly narrates, in different cities, to a nameless witness over some thirty years. And this nameless witness, also nervous, subject to breakdowns, psychic blindness, and depression, relays these narratives to the reader. Already we are overreading thirdhand accounts, or better, caught in the mazes of testimony. But try telling the testimony from the witness. Both suffer from symptoms of nerves, vague distress, aphasia, indisposition. Austerlitz, you see, is a collector of things that, for him, ward off awareness that his own narrative has gone missing, that his actions have lost their significance. It is the witness who narrates both Austerlitz and all that comes between them:

> During the pauses in our conversation we both noticed what an endless length of time went by before another minute had passed, and how alarming seemed the movement of that hand, which resembled a sword of justice, even though we were expecting it every time it jerked forward, slicing off the next one-sixtieth of an hour from the future and coming to a halt with such a menacing quiver that one's heart almost stopped. (8–9)

Excruciating time is the third protagonist.

In his sixtieth year, Austerlitz remembers that he was, in fact, trying all this time to forget. In 1939, as a very young child, perhaps at the age of four and a half, he was sent by his parents to England, traveling on a children's transport from Czechoslovakia. And he narrates this meeting of the past and present, where forgetting and remembering touch:

> I was listening to two women talking to each other about the summer of 1939, when they were children and had been sent to England on a special transport. They mentioned a number of cities ... only then did I know beyond any doubt that these fragments of memory were part of my own life as well. I was too alarmed by this sudden revelation ... (141)

Is history, then, what one overhears when it is least expected? Or is history the thing that comes after?

Again, Sebald (2003) would try to narrate another history, this time what he will call "the natural history of destruction." Try to imagine as testimony to war, he asks, cities devastated by bombs, and architectural ruins. And try to conceptualize the emotional dissociation that will resist the obligation of the witness. Sebald's lecture titled "Air War and Literature" is made from a montage of words and photographs, and the lecture resides in the time of what occurred and in the occurrence of its forgetting. Almost sixty years later, Sebald questions the meanings of official and unofficial silences toward the destruction of German cities from 1941 to 1945. He knows how words fail yet insists that this inadequacy of language to its object must still become the fragile stuff for ethical memory. His idea startles: to remember means going beyond individual stories of a defeated nation's suffering, that these stories of suffering are also made from the painful encounter with not being able to learn. Let us try, he seems to say, to understand the repression of this defeat, the apathy of history, the defeat of memory itself. And let us try to understand how this defeat, today, works within German suffering.

Sebald's lecture must pass through so many defenses against a psychical trauma of a defeated nation—civilian and prisoner-of-war survivors—after the Nazi defeat. He speaks about Christian Germans, those who supported the Third Reich, lived in German cities, and who probably believed in the Aryan nation. He does not speak directly of concentration camp survivors, or of the mass humanity destroyed there. These devastating facts form the background for the lecture and are needed to raise the question of the return of what could not be thought. He is referring to the after effects of defeat contained in the German citizen's postwar silence—or in a different context, what Baer (2002) called, in her memoir, "the baffling discrepancy between the world's terrible accusations and the strange aloofness of the people immediately affected" (166). Long after the war ended Baer remembers differently her own internment in a prisoner-of-war camp. She was part of the mass civilian internment beginning in 1945 by the Allied forces. Interned were those associated with the Nazi regime. These included ordinary civilians without moral qualms: teachers, doctors, architects, lawyers, students, and citizens spying and informing on other citizens. Their ages spanned from late adolescence to the elderly, an army of despondent citizens made from the ruins of men and women.

Sebald's lecture, however, looks to another dimension of the moral failure, allied to the individual dissociation but also belonging to those who have a chance of influencing, or better awakening, the post war public from its fractured memory. The idea may be that those who should know better should have acted differently. Yet they, too, were affected. Sebald is interested in the failure of artists and writers, wondering about the relation between aesthetics and ethics, with why, despite a few exceptions, there was such a silence on the part of German intelligentsia. Like Baer's memoir, although not in first person, his lecture, too, reads like an industrial anthropology rebuilt from the wreckage of its twisted and now rotting discarded content. There is Sebald sifting through found objects: aerial photographs of ravaged cities, bits of reports, found photographs, aging reminiscences. Why, he asks repeatedly, was the documentation and public discussion of the immensity of the destruction of the German cities and its chaotic afterwardness so minor that it appears to disappear from review? What is it about the defeat of the German people that is so shameful, that, if spoken at all, was only in done in secret? Why, if it is spoken, is it accompanied by bitterness and anger toward its victims' memories? What is the nature of a persecuted memory, made paranoid and tiny? Why is the discussion on what occurred for German citizens during those twelve years of Nazi dictatorship just now being brought to bear on the weight of historical consciousness? And how does the disappearance of the negativity of time matter to what can be learned today?

For Sebald, if any understanding is to be made, all these questions must be seen as interrelated. And thinking of these questions as a moral complex might allow for insight into that other anxiety that now composes what many call 'collective guilt,' where part of the defense against insight is that any lesson, any guilt, and any implication is too much for individual consciousness to bear. Indeed, consciousness, as Freud (1915) suggested during Germany's first war, becomes the exception. There will be disavowal or the refusal to think from traumatic events. What follows is something ordinary: there will be denial, claims that the event never happened. Meaninglessness will defend against memory, even become a substitute for it. I think Sebald is suggesting that the refusal, the fear, and the hatred of insight that parades in the form of opinions or forgetting, must also become part of memory's exploration. Our present responsibility is to encounter what has been disclaimed because memory is not a passive impression, nor is it even a receptacle of events that can be retrieved through the proper question or stimulation. Memory resists.

The details of the twelve-year Reich are immense, scattered now in archives, in memories, in museums, in documents, in material objects, and in missing art, for instance. I encountered many details that stopped my heart; for instance, in Baer's (2002) memoir where she mentions her first affiliation with the Nazi Party: "In 1936 when membership in the National Socialist youth movement became mandatory for all youngsters over age ten" (151) and goes on to say that she eagerly joined, spent five years in it, and became disillusioned in an ordinary way, not so much so that she left it at the time but just enough disillusionment that it could become, fifty years later, something she would have to ponder with agony and, yes, work through. Her memoir does not change what happened, but it does permit her to finally become present to herself and think about her own thoughtlessness and history of woeful disregard. One might say that only now can her suffering bear meaning. This is where the difference emerges. Looking back on her own life, Baer begins to explore a terrific apathy having to do with her active refusal of meaning and significance and her willingness later to be caught in her generation's mantra of a negation of guilt: "I didn't know what was happening. Nobody knew anything" (151). Some psychoanalysts might describe this state as a psychic deadness, brought on by depression, and oddly becoming itself a need for depression, necessary to normalize the mind, to make ordinary, a hatred of the pain of thinking, to make ordinary dissociation. In psychic deadness, actions become repetitive and mindless; relations lose significance; there is anomie and meaninglessness. These are also the after affects of trauma, where significance itself goes missing. In Sebald's lecture as well, readers cannot avoid meeting the general deadness of the civilians who survived their cities' destruction. And Sebald's (2003) speculation, that the destruction of German cities "had not registered in the consciousness of the reemergent nation" (69), struck its listeners as correct. In the lecture's postscript, Sebald also reminds us of the backdrop of the German silence on the destruction of its cities: "This intoxicating vision of destruction coincides with the fact that the real pioneering achievements in bomb warfare—Guernica, Warsaw, Belgrade, Rotterdam—were the work of the Germans" (104). To think about the destruction of German cities, Sebald concludes, these facts must be made to coincide, there must be a terrible association. What came before the destruction of German cities was the German military aerial war and its destruction of those other cities.

Some may ask why read in this archive, where the more the details accumulate the less sure we are of what education may now mean. This, too, is the fate of another sort of stranger, obligated to think within history and be affected. How are we to remember the ways the disturbances of love and hate, rivalry and loss, and disappointment and loneliness become our history? Can naming the 20th century as the psychoanalytic one influence our feelings today?

Bibliography

Adorno, Theodor W. (1959) 2002. *Kant's Critique of Pure Reason*. Edited by Rolf Tiedemann. Translated by Rodney Livingstone. Stanford, CA: Stanford University Press.
Arendt, Hannah. 1993. "The Crisis of Education." In *Between Past and Future: Eight Exercises in Political Thought*, 173–96. New York: Penguin Books.
Babel, Isaac. 2002. *The Complete Works of Isaac Babel*. Edited by Nathalie Babel. Translated by Peter Costantine. New York: W. W. Norton and Company.
Baer, Gertrud Mackprang. 2002. *In the Shadow of Silence: From Hitler Youth to Allied Internment: A Young Woman's Story of Truth and Denial*. Toronto: HarperCollins.
Brabant, Eva, Falzeder, Ernst, and Patrizia Giampieri-Deutsch, eds. 1992. *The Correspondence of Sigmund Freud and Sándor Ferenczi, vol. 1, 1908–1914*. Translated by Peter T. Hoffer. Cambridge, MA: The Belknap Press of Harvard University Press.
———. 1996. *The Correspondence of Sigmund Freud and Sándor Ferenczi, vol. 2, 1914–1919*. Translated by Peter T. Hoffer. Cambridge, MA: The Belknap Press of Harvard University Press.

———. 2000. *The Correspondence of Sigmund Freud and Sándor Ferenczi, vol. 3, 1920–1933*. Translated by Peter T. Hoffer. Cambridge, MA: The Belknap Press of Harvard University Press.
Freud, Sigmund. 1953–1974. *The Standard Edition of the Complete Psychological Works of Sigmund Freud*, edited and translated by James Strachey, in collaboration with Anna Freud. 24 vols. London: Hogarth Press and Institute for Psychoanalysis.
———. 1915. "Thoughts for the Times on War and Death." In *The Standard Edition of the Complete Psychological Works of Sigmund Freud*, edited and translated by James Strachey, in collaboration with Anna Freud, vol. 14, 273–301. London: Hogarth Press and Institute for Psychoanalysis.
Kristeva, Julia. 1991. *Strangers to Ourselves*. Translated by Leon S. Roudiez. New York: Columbia University Press.
———. 2001a. *Hannah Arendt*. Translated by Ross Guberman. New York: Columbia University Press.
———. 2001b. *Melanie Klein*. Translated by Ross Guberman. New York: Columbia University Press.
———. 2002. *Intimate Revolt: The Powers and Limits of Psychoanalysis, Vol 2*. Translated by Jeanine Herman. New York: Columbia University Press.
———. 2004. *Colette*. Translated by Jane Marie Todd. New York: Columbia University Press.
Roth, Joseph. 2001. *The Wandering Jews*. Translated by Michael Hofmann. New York: W. W. Norton.
Sebald, W.G. 2001. *Austerlitz*. Translated by Anthea Bell. Toronto: Knopf Canada.
———. 2003. *On the Natural History of Destruction*. Translated by Anthea Bell. Toronto: Knopf Canada.

CHAPTER 8

Public Education as States of Mind[1]

IT IS DIFFICULT to decide when we speak of public education if we are dreaming of its future, mourning its past, or simply feeling the contentious force of its presence without knowing why. We surely know that almost everyone who passes through its many hallways leaves with a view of what public education is like and unlike. We leave with a view of a public that we are inextricably a part of. And if we listen carefully to what can be said of education, we might find in these sentiments an avalanche of mental attitudes toward the public such as what other people are like and unlike. And if we step back for a panorama view, we might then imagine contentious debates with publics as education. One side is influenced by generations of families, teachers, and communities that pass on to the newly arrived contrary emotional convictions, anxious theories of learning, and fractured experience both for and against the need and desire for education. The other side involves instituted education as a constellation of inheritances made from what the social cannot resolve. That is, education as idea, experience, and outcome inherits disclaimed national histories and public conflicts of ill will. Expressions of these conflicts release a twofold dilemma for mental health: We all begin with the vulnerability of growing up in schools and, along the way, are charged with the continuing work of symbolizing unresolved history. I am considering the imaginary of public education as made from the mismatch between inner time, political life, generational conflict, and dreams of social transformations.

As for social transformations, there have been many. Since the early 1970s, public education has swayed between demands for human rights and the regressed history of segregation, between gender celebrations and sexual inequalities, between class divisions and racism. Whether we think of new inclusivity, diversity, or plurality, and whether we think about free expression and the right to proper sex education and birth control, we cannot settle what serves as the sources of education. Our questions become particularly urgent given that public education is charged with providing, due to de-institutionalization and desegregation, the right for children and adolescents with special needs to have the least restrictive environment that is education (Evans 2017). While this measure mainly belongs to special education, I believe it can be stretched to public life in education. The least restrictive education is tied to freedom of expression, sexuality, personhood, and public comity. These demands have certainly led to new rights for gay, lesbian, bisexual, transgender, queer, and two-spirit people. Through student-led movements, there are new demands for an education without fear of violence, without guns. As for curricular efforts, our pedagogies must grapple with creating closer ties to testimony, reconciliation, and social tolerance. Yet it is still difficult to decide how minds change, whether education changes society, and whether and why society changes education.

My sweeping observations also belong to inner time, and I ask that we imagine public education as a state of mind, dreamlike in its condensations and displacements, and ego-like in its fantasies, defenses, and desires. By this I mean that it is impossible to separate education in mind from the health of the public mind. And this raises the deep dilemma of how and whether public education can transform itself given its tendentious history and in present time, that today's public education enacts the conflicts of at least five interacting generations of public attitudes made from memories of great grandparents, grandparents, parents, adult children, and children's children.

The tentacles of instituted public education have a long reach. Its functions are never far from the courts and police, the social workers and psychologists, the prisons, the welfare system, the testing industry, and the guts and policies of political frameworks. In terms of the professions, we experience long-standing debates over whether teachers, administrators, and policy makers are up to the task. Then, too, there are significant questions as to whether universities can be trusted, whether teacher education is broken, and, indeed, whether public education creates a past or future.

These public antimonies have a personal side, touching not only what has happened to us in childhood and adolescence and what we thought happened to our parents. The antimonies also affect what we have witnessed or have refused to acknowledge that has happened to others. There is the education in mind and the education to be faced and changed. There is the public in mind and the public in transit and change. And it is this constellation I want to develop in my remarks, treating public education as an emotional situation, a challenge to language, and as a state of mind that involves an intimate link to mental health. I'll discuss emotional situations of public education through transitional scenes of inheriting a past one could not make, experiencing a present affected by what came before, and facing a future one can neither know nor predict. And I see these dynamics as constituting inner time and its conflicts with external affairs. I want to describe mental health from the vantage of what life is like when we try to express something of the self and the world and when we try to make sense of what has happened to the self and others.

Phantasies

I sometimes fantasize about public education as if it were a gigantic social thermometer, as if that would be a way to record how both education and the public are doing. This gigantic social thermometer would then give us some sense of degrees of social illness, degrees of failure, and degrees of good-enough stability. There would be higher and lower temperatures that register fevered states of public mental health or that assure us that so far, the patient is not burning. But the phantasy can go no further. Besides, the idea of public education cannot be a hermetically sealed instrument, and children and adolescents, even if they have no voting rights, take heat from the world of others they may not understand. Yet it may be useful to think of public education through its temperamental conflicts: as states of mind education is subject to failures, breakdowns, and, yes, the frustration of incompleteness. If so, we would then have to narrate public education's role in national histories of woeful disregard and then through narratives of reparation become sensitized to how new generations receive and work through what has already happened. We would also need to open histories of discovery and shock: of family secrets and social denial of mental pain and psychical reality. We would have to begin from our uneven development and create new narratives that help us say more about the challenges of creating an open, public society. We would need to accept the challenges and demands of wanting education.

There would have to be an interest in inner time. The psychoanalyst André Green (2016) provides an expansive notion of psychical temporality with his claim that the historical, or what has happened, is hard to handle because it is a work in progress and affected by regression accompanied by phantasy, defense, negation, and desire. Green describes the historical as "what has happened; what has not happened; what could have happened; what has happened to someone else but not me; what could not have happened; and ... a statement that one would not have even dreamed of as a representation of what really happened" (2–3). I think these oppositional dynamics of wish and reality and denial and testimony are also the stakes for new narratives of public education.

Even as public education is mostly portrayed from the side of its bureaucratic tendencies enacted by administrative mentality, experiencing its affecting conditions is made more intimate and surprising by the reach of meanings we can give to mental health. The turn I want to take—what I see as affecting concerns underway—begins with relating public education to our reparative capacities. I see this work as involving our handling of knowledge and social belonging with the promises of care and toleration. I imagine the possibility of experiencing education as the fragile threading of the social bond and a necessary condition for a generous public. These lines of development emerge from those who have been harmed by administered national history, the obscurity of bureaucratic vocabulary, and the disavowal of systemic violence and its woeful disregard of human rights. The new demand is for a public that wants more education and desires new ways to experience the freedom to think, feel, and repair.

Secrets As 'Half-Knowledge'

What has happened to experience in public education could not have occurred overnight; the details of change first signal back to social agony and its denial before protests and new questions revision what has happened. When the Catholic pope traveled to Ireland in late August 2018, he did not come to apologize for the church history of criminal activity. But he did come to a new, unfamiliar country, one that challenges generations of cruelty within church authority. The Ireland the pope met is a country that speaks legally of its tortuous silences. Such changes cannot spring full blown; there had to be a long history of creative literature, art, theater, music, and protest that began the affective work of untangling the mind from the compulsions of the denial of bodily life. With an awakening of public awareness and testimony by those who have suffered, we may link the ravages made from scandals of sexual child abuse by the church to the revelations of girls expelled to laundries of slave labor and to the unmarked graves of babies and the stolen children taken from single women. These acknowledged generations of history can also be understood as the basis for wanting rights to gay and lesbian marriage, legal abortion, sex education, and to a public education dedicated to protecting the mind.

When public education is brought closer to experiencing transformations in human rights, its own right is to become part of the world. Here I see the work of changing minds as involved in affecting mental health. For when there is the possibility of protection of bodily freedom, when the lockstep of conformity and compliance loses its footing, then, the situations of social transformation become beholden to the right to have one's mind, imagination, and mental health. But the problem is that education then involves us all in coming to terms with histories of bad faith and working through even a hatred of having to change. The other part of this transformation concerns creating new narratives that both acknowledge shattered lives and urge the movements toward reparative pedagogies. All of this includes disruptive thinking that disquiets imagination.

To learn from the failures of the social, one has to be willing to experience what I have called "difficult knowledge" (Britzman 1998), an emotional situation that occurs before we are ready to understand and that charges us to stand mental pain that impresses meaning yet to be made. As I was preparing for my visit to Maynooth University, I came across a startling essay by Clair Wills (2018), King Edward VII Professor of English Literature at Cambridge University. It was published in August 2018 in the *New York Review of Books* under the title "Family Secrets." She wrote of her three generations of rural Irish family history and struggled with the long reach of national and family cover stories that disclaimed or perhaps could not remember the wreckage of lives lived and lost. Her essay was about trying to know something of a past felt before known while learning to narrate with greater feelings the relations between her life and those cut short. Wills writes that she "came of age as a generation as the inheritors of a history we half-knew, and the consequences of that half-knowledge were unpredictable" (14). What she could not know was how her family, years later, felt about their tragic past, then and now. That, too, was Wills's "half knowledge." It was with her knowledge of the past that she came to understand why her mother's generation seemed to her to settle for deep sadness rather than mirroring the grown-up outrage that Wills first felt upon learning what had happened to family members. Her view: "It is not what we know but how we know" (14).

"Family Secrets," began with Wills (2018) recounting the death of her three-day-old son in 1996. Her question was, What would it be to commemorate a child who did not exist but who was born? Her personal question led Wills to remember many others: those who are, she wrote, buried in "the unconsecrated graveyards that dot the Irish countryside . . . home to unbaptized babies but also to criminals, suicides, and the insane" (10). Willis was also asking what of today's generation that inherits "industrial schools, country homes, the asylums, the laundries, and the Mother and Baby Homes" (10)? Her answer: "Nearly everyone over the age of forty knows of someone who was incarcerated in one of those institutions, if only for a time. Nowadays, blogs, advice columns, and chat rooms online reveal thousands of people searching for information about their mothers, sisters, aunts, and, weirdly, even about themselves" (10). While not explicitly stated, "nearly everyone" includes those who oversee public education: teachers, administrators, government agents, welfare workers, religious orders, and university professors.

Beyond the school walls, people searched for buried or repressed history through social mechanisms of publication—the blogs, advice columns, and searches for one's parents, siblings, and children. Much of the search involved the fog of not remembering, and that, too, became part of the stories. These efforts find their way into public education, provided that we want more education and provided that we want new modes of belonging that lean upon searching narratives. They are the counterpoints to populist pressures for closure and denial and giving air to reparative urges. They take the side of history closer to how André Green (2016) described relational ties: "what we never dreamed of as a representation of what has happened" (3).

For good and for bad, public education intimately affects the course of mental life in its unpredictability. To think of public education with mental health, we would have to imagine the inner world of emotions as both statements of needs yet to be met and as an address to a desire for relationality. To think this way with our thoughts, fears, hostilities, anxieties, and wishes, we would have to get to know something more about how these ephemeral affects are transmitted and communicated not only as political positions but also more intimately and more personally, as states of mind. There is after all the changing nature between psychical and material reality, then the mismatch of inner time with social learning, and then symbolizing "how we know" the ways in which relationality is transmitted, apprehended, perceived, and dreamed of.

Mental Health

I think we can say that public education appeals to anxiety, fantasies, and desires; to the past as if it can ensure the future; and to the gap between inner time and external reality. We can ask whether, for example, school structures, modes of authority, and daily interactions are felt as care for vulnerability, dependency, and doubt or whether these daily interactions are persecutory, frightening, and humiliating. And these situations do affect whether mental health can be considered as elemental to the creation of public life that desires narratives of reparation and, I think, a desire for an education with the least restrictions.

How difficult it is, however, to consider the material world experienced as states of mind. We are, after all, subjects both to our own mind and to the minds of others. And this relationality, felt as emotional atmosphere, opens for me the question of how we might create affecting views of pluralities of mental health that can accommodate the ups and downs of psychical life. I have found two soft definitions that follow the measure of least restrictive approach. From the vantage of illness, suffering, emotional distress, and isolation, the British psychoanalyst, John Rickman, told D. W. Winnicott (1996): "Mental illness consists in not being able to find anyone who can stand you" (218). Winnicott offered this view in one of his talks to social workers and educators. I think that isolation and loneliness is a prevalent experience in public education as it is in everyday life and, in not finding anyone, one is only left to one's primal agonies (Winnicott [1963] 1992).

A different direction belongs to Alain Ehrenberg's (2016) history of how the idea of a psychological self has affected our understanding of personhood and, I would add, how the idea of a psychological self affects public education. Ehrenberg conceives of the Janus face of mental health as belonging to personal development and social tolerance. Mental health, Ehrenberg writes, challenges

> the essential elements of individualistic society, like self-value, the opposition between responsibility and illness, the ability to succeed in life, the ability to educate one's children, and so on . . . [and as] the springboard of thinking and communication skills, learning, emotional growth, resilience, and self-esteem. (xiv)

Mental health involves mental pain such as depression, anxiety, and fragmentation *and* becomes our means to grasp these complications made from belonging, interest, and thinking (Klein 1975). I think a great deal leans on the links of mental health and a good life dependent on a civic culture capable of enjoying plurality, thinking in times of conflict, and modifying frustration and anxiety with new knowledge.

Thinking at Odds

So what is thinking as tied to human rights and, to enlarge the question, what is thinking for the right to be human? The first metaphor belongs to the philosopher Hannah Arendt (2018), "thinking without a banister" (473). The second belongs to the psychoanalyst Wilfred Bion's (1993) "thoughts exist without a thinker" and "thoughts awaiting thinkers" (165). His (1993) idea is "[t]hinking has to be called into existence to cope with thoughts" (111). Both formulations of thinking from Bion emerge from exasperation, uncertainty, frustration, and a search for significance. Thinking is rooted in emotional situations of being *without* something needed and noticing absence, estrangement, and creativity.

Arendt's (2018) metaphor, "thinking without a banister," came later in her life (473). She was sixty-six years old and spoke of this idea in 1972 at York University in Toronto. It does seem to be a message sent to our time, and in the work of Sharon Sliwinski (2005), such dreamlike stories open human rights to its intimacy and agony. Arendt insists that thinking occurs with the things that cannot be figured out. Here is her description of what for her thinking is like:

> I have a metaphor . . . which I never published but kept for myself. I call it thinking without a banister. In German, "*Denken ohne Geländer.*" That is, as you go up and down the stairs you can always hold on to the banister so that you don't fall down. But we have lost this banister. That is the way I tell it to myself. And this is indeed what I try to do. (2018, 473)

She called her work "tentative thinking," and it seems to me the symposium so long ago enacted a particular quality of trying to speak of public education and what it is we have to do to risk our own fragility to create more than what we have received.

I found the transcript of Arendt's (2018) symposium painful to read for Arendt was defending the freedom to think with the tentative kind of thinking she was doing. She had to acknowledge that her thinking was subject to failing, to almost falling, to tripping, and to losing her footing. Perhaps for these reasons Arendt did not want to indoctrinate. At one point in the symposium, she referred to her university teaching. She said she only wished to "rouse or awaken my students" (449). And in this sense, the key distinction she proposed is that the opposite of thinking is thoughtlessness. The thoughtlessness that Arendt had in mind that day had to do with the denial of the fact of plurality in the world. "I would say that any society that has lost respect for thinking is not in good shape" (450).

Here is where I think Bion's views open onto the crossroad of public education. How and why we think does matter. Bion (1994) was interested in tolerating mental pain and he understands thinking as thinking over an emotional experience that "cannot be conceived in isolation from a relationship" (43). These relations are emotional matters of love, hate, and knowledge. Bion concludes: "The choice that matters to the psycho-analyst is one that lies between *procedures designed to evade frustration and those designed to modify it. That is the crucial decision*" (29, italics in original). Educators have the same choice and crisis.

Is Public Education Impossible?

Freud's ([1925] 1968) psychoanalytic view proposed three impossible professions: governance, medicine, and education. These are also impossible institutions as they give direction to others just at the point when these professions are affected by what is most unknown about life. The impossibility is not only that we have trouble following directions. I think when things do not go according to policy and plan and evidence, professionals have the new problem of understanding quite differently the sways of relationality oriented by the tensions between helplessness, dependency, and autonomy. We can never leave the human sphere and the professions as well are subject to depression, anxiety, and denial of psychical reality. And yet the impossible professions can also aim for self-activity, and much of it has to do with the provisions of education.

Castoriadis (1994) opens the problem of pedagogy by way of its paradox: "Pedagogy has at every age to develop the self-activity of the subject by using, so to speak this very self-activity. The point of pedagogy is not to teach particular things, but to develop in the subject the capacity to learn: learn to learn, learn to discover, learn to invent" (6). And yet there are ideas to teach, events to learn from, histories to make sense of, silences to narrate, and denials to explore. The capacity to learn is intimately bound to the right to narrate, not only to tell a story but also to create a story from the stream of experience. Castoriadis suggests this work is filled with uncertainty and proposes the antimony of education: "to help in creating autonomy for their subjects by using an autonomy which does not yet exist.... To be sure, human reality exceeds this logic" (6).

The same uncertainty can be lent to the idea of the public: creating a public that does not exist but that could and that could imagine autonomy as becoming and as yet to come. I think this approach also touches upon the work of Carl Anders Söfström (2018), who has designated as "livable life" both mind and heart in the service of new states of mind. But this means that that there can be no education without crisis and the question of crisis is also a question of the crisis of meaning.

On the matter of law, psychoanalysis proposes that the law joins prohibition and desire, provided that it is fair and on the side of thinking. The law is found not only in one's name, within the family and the incest taboo, but also in the desire to become a speaking subject, to communicate, to serve psychical freedom, and to care for the other and the self. It is the law of the difference between generations and the links of authority with love. And given that public education is so intimately expressing a notion of law, we can turn to Kristeva (2010):

> the Law we are talking about is a symbolic act that prohibits, slows, and limits while at the same time inaugurating a new psychical action. On what condition? On the condition that this symbolic act, this Law, tell the truth of desire: in other words, that it be accurate, that is to say, formulated in such a way that the subject is capable of appropriating it so as to be reborn at a given moment ... (171)

In other words, the law cannot be insane. By insanity I mean the ferocious destruction and loss of narratives, a dismissal of the difficult and ongoing work of interpreting right from wrong, and a paranoid proclivity to splitting and humiliation. By insanity I mean the denial that every education inherits the insanity of its national past and has the task of remembering and working through rather than repeating and acting out past traumas and humanly induced destruction. And by insanity I also mean something utterly ordinary that D.W. Winnicott (2001) pointed to as a quality of madness, first by acknowledging that every human experiences "the strain of relating inner and outer reality" (13) and then, given this tension, proposed a challenge to reality testing: "Should an adult make claims on us for our acceptance of the objectivity of his subjective phenomena we discern or diagnose madness" (14).

Affecting Concerns Under Way

It is difficult to define mental health with the least restrictions, and the same goes for a notion of "cure." Cure is not the restoration of an earlier state of health but can be thought of as a situation where one now handles new challenges. Ehrenberg's (2016) discussion of the changing modes of depression found at the end of the twentieth century, raised the problem of cure as a question for pedagogy. He drew on George Canguilhem, who recommended that doctors engage a pedagogy of cure. What could be taught? "This pedagogy should work to help the subject understand that no technique, no institution, present or future, can provide him with the guaranteed integrity of his relational powers with other people and things" (quoted in Ehrenberg 2016, 202). The integrity has more to do with affective life underway, but that too depends on others. Ehrenberg, whom I discussed earlier as presenting the idea of the Janus face of mental health, also proposed the complication of understanding "cure": "There is no cure without work, without development, without a story—a fiction in which the person is involved through the use of the I" (202).

What brings together all these disparate emotional situations—public, education, mental health, reparation, thinking, and cure—is the capacity to tell a story that changes how the story can be told, that changes the 'I' who narrates, the 'You' who is witness, and the 'Us' it creates, and that proposes a story of questions as to how one comes to know. And these stories are also the means to understand, a little better, the mismatch between inner time and the challenges of social imagination. The psychoanalyst Melanie Klein (1975) called this work of losing and regaining, "the pain of integration" (304). But here, I think we are struggling with the pain of incompleteness and the ways we may handle stories of absence and presence as affecting concerns underway.

Bibliography

Arendt, Hannah. 2018. *Thinking without a Banister: Essays in Understanding, 1953–1975*. Edited by Jerome Kohn. New York: Schocken Press.
Bion, Wilfred R. 1993. *Second Thoughts*. London: Karnac Books.
———. 1994. *Learning from Experience*. London: Jason Aronson Inc.

Britzman, Deborah P. 1998. *Lost Subjects, Contested Objects: Toward a Psychoanalytic Inquiry of Learning*. Albany: State University of New York Press.

Castoriadis, Cornelius. 1994. "Psychoanalysis and Politics." In *Speculations after Freud: Psychoanalysis, Philosophy and Culture*, edited by Sonu Shamdasani and Michael Münchow, 2–12. London: Routledge.

Ehrenberg, Alain. 2016. *The Weariness of the Self: Diagnosing the History of Depression in the Contemporary Age*. Translated by Enrico Caouette, Jacob Homel, David Homel, and Don Winkler, under the direction of David Homel. Montreal and Kingston: McGill-Queen's University Press.

Evans, Bonnie. 2017. *The Metamorphosis of Autism: A History of Child Development in Britain*. Manchester, UK: Manchester University Press.

Freud, Sigmund. (1925) 1968. "Preface to Aichhorn's *Wayward Youth*." In *The Standard Edition of the Complete Psychological Works of Sigmund Freud, Volume XIX (1923–1925): The Ego and the Id and Other Works*, edited and translated by James Strachey, in collaboration with Anna Freud, 271–76. London: Hogarth Press.

Green, André. 2016. "Experience and Thinking in Analytic Practice." In *André Green at the Squiggle Foundation*, edited by Jan Abram, 1–15. London: Karnac Books.

Klein, Melanie. 1975. *Envy and Gratitude & Other Works 1946–1963*. London: Hogarth Press.

Kristeva, Julia. 2010. *Hatred and Forgiveness*. Translated by Jeanine Herman. New York: Columbia University Press.

Söfström, Carl Anders. 2018. "Livable Life, Educational Theory and the Imperative of Constant Change." *European Educational Research Journal* 17 (5): 621–30.

Sliwinski, Sharon. 2005. "Thinking without Banisters: Toward a Compassionate Inquiry into Human Rights Education." *Educational Theory* 55 (2): 219–30.

Wills, Clair. 2018. "Family Secrets." *New York Review of Books*, August 16.

Winnicott, Donald W. (1963) 1992. "Fear of Breakdown." In *Psychoanalytic Explorations*, edited by Clare Winnicott, Ray Shepherd, and Madeleine Davis, 87–95. Cambridge, MA: Harvard University Press.

———. 1996. "The Mentally Ill in Your Caseload." In *The Maturational Processes and the Facilitating Environment: Studies in the Theory of Emotional Development*, 217–29. Madison, CT: International Universities Press.

———. 2001. *Playing and Reality*. New York: Brunner-Routledge.

Endnotes

1 This chapter was originally titled, "Affecting Concerns Under Way: Public education as matters of mental health," and was given as keynote to Maynooth Educational Forum 2018–The Publicness of Education in our Republic at Maynooth University, Kildare Ireland.

CHAPTER 9

'Each To Each' And The Equality of Vulnerability

"What do you see? What do you think about it? What do you make of it?" These are the founding questions Rancière's (1991) 18th-century ignorant schoolmaster, Jacotot, proposes to pedagogy dedicated to the presupposition of equality of intellect and so taking instruction from the subject as capable of putting together her or his own thoughts (23). Without this assumption of an equality of intellect, there is only stultifying explication, isolation, inhibition, and a litany of negations. The schoolmaster's questions are a tonic to the will and lend faith to the idea that one can teach and learn what one does not know. "The problem," Rancière writes, "is to reveal an intelligence to itself" (29). And later he remarks that the communication of this intelligence requires translation or "the desire to understand and be understood" (63).

I consider these desires as emotional situations in waiting, as object relations in the making, and eventually, as a coming commentary on the vulnerabilities of selfhood with others. My suggestion is that we can put into words the work of revealing the significance of emotional life by acknowledging the fragile tie between the desire to understand and to feel one can be understood. For this special problem of recognition, one would have to notice meaninglessness: times when thoughts fall apart, when experience loses its foothold in the world of others, and when social denial obliterates a second chance. How others translate this loss, this affective excess, and understand their transference to this estrangement, decides whether political life can admit the vulnerability, diversity, and significance of the emotional world as always necessary to the social bond. I hope to give value to the nature of this affected dialogue and open Rancière's (1991) formulation of equality—"each to each"—to the equality of vulnerability.

I want to make a case for considering, alongside consciousness, a prior formative experience, namely, the dependency on the psychical world that creates not only the wish for equality of intellect but also the defenses made from anxiety over its loss. A psychoanalytic view of intersubjective life begins with a constitutive inequality that is called "helplessness," or asymmetrical learning relations conveyed through unconscious phantasies, defenses, and desires and that go on to impress the emotional situations of childhood, family, schools, and experiences of generational difference. These object relations of inexperience, authority, and knowledge are subject to a failure of translation. How the subject makes sense of having a body, how other bodies come to be loved and hated, and why these matters of "each to each" are unspeakable and foreclosed in the social imaginary—configure an intersubjective dilemma. For psychoanalysis, the ethics of therapeutic action may only emerge from putting to words emotional situations in order to bear the weight and anxiety of asymmetrical relations, dependency, vulnerability, and uneven development.

To illustrate these concerns, I turn to Kristeva's (2010) understanding of psychic vulnerability and present some clinical snippets of Joyce McDougall's (McDougall and Lebovici 1969) account of a child's analysis, *Dialogue with Sammy*. McDougall and her patient, "Sammy," allows me to ask, What may the human condition of vulnerability give to the idea of "each to each"? I chose this case for its commentary on education and dependency, for its discussion of intersubjectivity as emerging from the clash of words, for how McDougall finds significance to the shared dilemma of not understanding yet wishing to know, for the ways the analyst is affected by her work with others, and for the psychoanalytic theory of transference that peppers the social bond with an unconscious history of love and hate. We find here our vulnerability to language and the other through an interest in the convolutions of psychical life and its affects: anxiety, compliance, resistance, attacks on linking, hostility, and ideality. From the ripples of events, there can emerge the containment of thinking and a renewed curiosity toward actualizing intellect with significance, meaning, and the other (e.g., Bion 1994; Britzman 2011; Joseph 2000; Kristeva 2007, 2011).

The Right to a Symbolic

"Disabilities," Kristeva (2011) writes in a letter to the French government, "are multiple—motor, sensory, psychical, mental—and singular" (29). She continues: "What cannot be shared is the disabled person's "exposure to a discrimination" (29). The minimal remedy is for social policies to refuse to repeat discrimination; that policy becomes affected by the provision for care of the self. Kristeva is well aware she is speaking for others excluded from the symbolic realm. But when speaking for the rights of her own child, Kristeva must accept this risk with the idea that vulnerabilities, while belonging to life, are deeply defended against and acted out as a hatred of weakness and dependency. Her faith is just as demanding: "My ambition, my utopia, consists of believing that this vulnerability reflected in the disabled person forms us deeply, if you prefer, unconsciously and that as a result, it can be shared" (30). As a psychoanalyst, her passion is with listening to what, for each of us, is "irremediable" (44). And with this insistence, the French spirit of universality becomes urgent through its missing link. So she rewrote the 18th-century revolutionary slogan into this: "Liberty, Equality, Fraternity and . . . Vulnerability."

What drives "each to each"—Rancière's (1991) critical formulation that ties equality of intellect to the acts of literacy and education—is libidinal: affective bonds of care, dependency, and desire subject to both the unconscious and to language, all that can be welcomed. Kristeva (2010) articulates a paradoxical demand, "respect for a vulnerability that cannot be shared" (30), but that may become so. Her and our defense of the human condition as the right to the symbolic leans upon asymmetry: our dependency on others and on words as a creative solution to the Real. Care for the emotional world and its vulnerable meaning is prior to and a condition for what Rancière (1991) calls the equality of the intellect.

For Rancière (1991) words that may not be understood but can be recognized as communication are the essential link of the social bond, provided that one word affects another word and that this linking carries with meaning a constitutive fragmentation or alienation that language supposes. In brief, for Rancière, the philosopher, the architecture of the social can be made from assuming the equality of intellect; for Kristeva, the psychoanalyst, this architecture of intellect is fragile and can suffer. Kristeva's claim for a new spirit of equality leans upon the complexities of psychical life and the chance to express anxieties made from what the human must share and lose. The human is always subject to the uncertainties of bios, logos, Eros, and ethnos and to the ambiguity of having to interpret reality and translate the affected psychical body, composed and compromised by health and illness and by the urgency of becoming a subject with and for others.

The Dictator And The Ignorant Analyst

Sammy Y. was nine-and-a-half years old when his parents moved from the United States to Paris and brought him to Joyce McDougall, a child analyst. McDougall's (McDougall and Lebovici 1969) account is already a circus of language. The analysis was conducted in English, originally written in French, and later translated into English. It is the first lengthy published narrative of a child analysis. The frame follows their eight months of work through 166 sessions, five days a week. The analysis came to a sudden end when Sammy's parents sent him back to the United States to attend a residential school that specialized in the treatment of schizophrenia, a difficult diagnosis subject to a history of psychiatric debate and, for those involved in its terrors, heartbreak (Leader 2011).

Sammy set the singular conditions for both the analysis and the book that would follow. He said, "I am the dictator, take my dictations" (McDougall and Lebovici 1969, 1). McDougall was ordered to be the silent scribe, the ignorant analyst. And in the beginning, Sammy dictated his bizarre world and McDougall was only allowed to read his exact words back to him. It was not until the 78th session that Sammy began to write alongside McDougall. Before that, McDougall accepted the position of the ignorant scribe and accompanied Sammy into his emotional storms.

By the fourth session, McDougall writes a note to herself: "He gives the impression of being under the sway of a terrifying fantasy whose intensity disturbs his capacity to communicate" (McDougall and Lebovici 1969, 24). In the fifth session, after Sammy dictates a violent story of a magic face that can do anything it wants, McDougall writes, "At times he is using words as objects rather than as a means for communication" (31). She also realizes that she, the analyst, is the magic face and must hold in her writing all of his bad feelings. Sammy, she believes, has given up on the external world. In the tenth session, McDougall gives an interpretation: "Sammy, I think you are telling me that you have many troubled thoughts in which everything is sad or breaking up and you are afraid I can't do a thing to help you" (39). His reply is to scream out numbers, list more chapters in his story, and order her to shut up.

The sessions are harrowing to read. Sammy refuses McDougall's thoughts and complains he is bored. He demands more toys. He screams when she makes the slightest movements and continually demands matches to light. He throws water at her and kicks over the furniture. Sometimes he strikes her. McDougall only asks Sammy to use words. But there is no meeting between Sammy's preoccupation with his body and the words he hurtles. His elaborate narratives are full of sexual violence, murder, and angry shit. Eating is the same as being murdered. Many of his stories end with desperate threats. Often when the session is over, Sammy refuses to leave. McDougall has to carry him out. In the first five weeks of analysis, he bites her, blows on her cheeks, demands that she only take down his words, tries to see her breasts, and wishes her to be naked. By the 24th session, McDougall reflects on her helplessness and Sammy's mounting aggression. She changes her approach, brings into the room the toys Sammy has asked for, and takes his lead. In the next session, Sammy destroys all of the new toys.

By the 35th session, Sammy wishes "Dougie" to read his story back to him, yet warns her, "Don't read it as though you are in love with your husband!" (McDougall and Lebovici 1969, 76). He becomes preoccupied with her other patients and wishes to be the only one. But he also begins to ask her to read her thoughts about his story and tell him what he is thinking. This is a delicate task; often his sessions are filled with a torrent of words that seem to destroy themselves. Months later, McDougall will give a name to such talk: this is Sammy's special language. In session 63, McDougall begins to think with Sammy's wish to contain meaning and shares his hope that her pen will not fail.

Slowly, hints of dialogue emerge. In session 106 Sammy tells Dougie that everything is terribly sad, even the buildings are giving him frowns. McDougall says, "Perhaps there are bits of your own feeling that you've put on to the buildings and things outside you. "Sammy replies, "This worries me. Do other people have these ideas too? It's bad, isn't it?" And, McDougall mirrors his view: "You seem to think that to have feelings is bad." Sammy replies, "Yes, I do. Is it all right to feel things? Does it happen to other people?" (McDougall and Lebovici 1969, 178). McDougall writes in summary: "I tell him there are many ways of imagining things; that many people do it, and we call it 'day-dreaming' because we realize that these things are not true. Sammy is most interested and happy to hear this" (179).

A few sessions later Sammy asks McDougall why he talks in a funny way. McDougall responds: "Yes, sometimes you use a sort of 'special talking.' Can you tell me more about it yourself?" (McDougall and Lebovici 1969, 183). It is not until session 112 that McDougall tells Sammy when he is involved in his "special talking" and that this talk has replaced the work of fantasy and play. Along with the special talking, McDougall gives other names to Sammy's speech. There are "thinking troubles" and "dream-feelings," both an index of times when he feels far away from the world.

The analysis has ups and downs, and both are needed. Most steady is McDougall's capacity to be with Sammy. She learns from him how to share his sense of his inner world. She also records her own difficulties in controlling herself during Sammy's tantrums, insults, and hitting. Most notable is that she is able to transform her practices in order to create a relationship founded on her transference to his words.

Near the end of their work, Sammy asks if one only has troubles to bring to the analyst. They are listening to Sammy's choice of a recording of the Brandenburg Concerto:

> J.M.—Everything that you talk about is interesting in analysis. It doesn't have to be a trouble. Today you have told me your ideas about all kinds of things as you thought you felt like having a friendly talk rather than being a patient with 'troubles', and perhaps also it's a way of proving that you can be like this with me without feeling that you're in any danger.
>
> S. —Maybe I wanted to have music today so as not to be a patient! . . . I think the music helped me to talk. (McDougall and Lebovici 1969, 222–23)

The calmness of the session is unusual, and in the last sessions before Sammy leaves, more terrors ensue and McDougall is in doubt about offering any interpretations, as he may need to speak of these terrors in order to manage his sense of loss. McDougall is left wondering how people who have no troubles at all can ever meet Sammy's troubling thoughts.

Yes, at times, Sammy begins to realize the difference between his terrors and the world beyond them, and yet he may need these terrors to even notice the world and think that his horrible thoughts cannot be omnipotent even as they feel this way. Their last session is filled with sadness and comes to an abrupt end. Sammy's parents send him to a residential school, and McDougall acknowledges to Sammy that he feels abandoned by her. It is an extraordinary good-bye, and the next day Sammy left for his new school.

A Path For Free Association?

In an interview with himself, Rancière (2009) describes his method as a path, or an "intervention in specific contexts" (114). His interest is in how words stage a scene, "things that the speaker and those who hear it are invited to share—as spectacle, a feeling, a phrasing, a mode of intelligibility" (117). McDougall's discussion of Sammy proposes a different view: object things stage both our wish for words and our fear of them.

Kristeva (2000) has proposed psychoanalysis as a treatment of thought and words, needed to assume that the right to the symbolic invents a new relation that links our constitutive dependency with others to words, theirs and ours. This asymmetrical relation, she insists, qualifies the vulnerability of psychical life and its creative desire that there be meaning to suffering's war on words. In Kristeva's (2000) view,

> '[t]here is meaning': this will be my universal. And 'I' use words of the tribe to inscribe my singularity. Je est un autre ('I is another'): this will be my

difference, and 'I' will express my specificity by distorting the nevertheless necessary clichés of the codes of communication and by constantly deconstructing ideas/concepts/ideologies/ philosophies that "I" has inherited...

Other eras have had this experience. Its radicalness, however, is unique in our century, one of education and information. (19)

Can we now say, amidst the ideality of education and information and despite the war against the freedom of the mind, that there is another scene to respond to, another affecting equality that we know nothing about but nonetheless communicates what is most fragile and sad about the disparities of inheritance? Can we think about times when "each to each" signifies a psychic collapse and a war on language? The solution to the real also involves the news that because there is the unconscious, and because there is the other, there meaning becomes. And what would you make from this transference of psychical life as both constituting our vulnerability and dependent upon the face of the other?

Bibliography

Bion, Wilfred R. 1994. *Experiences in Groups and Other Papers*. New York: Routledge Press.
Britzman, Deborah P. 2011. *Freud and Education*. New York: Routledge Press.
Joseph, Betty. 2000. "Agreeableness as Obstacle." *International Journal of Psychoanalysis* 81 (4): 641–49.
Kristeva, Julia. 2000. *The Sense and Non-Sense of Revolt*. Translated by Jeanine Herman. New York: Columbia University Press.
———. 2007. "Adolescence, Syndrome of Ideality." *Psychoanalytic Review* 94 (5): 714–25.
———. 2010. "Liberty, Equality, Fraternity and . . . Vulnerability." In *Hatred and Forgiveness*, translated by Jeanine Herman, 29–45. New York: Columbia University Press.
Leader, Darien. 2011. *What Is Madness?* London: Penguin Group.
McDougall, Joyce and Serge Lebovici. 1969. *Dialogue with Sammy: A Psycho-Analytic Contribution to the Understanding of Child Psychosis*. New York: International University Press.
Rancière, Jacques. 1991. *The Ignorant Schoolmaster: Five Lessons in Intellectual Emancipation*. Translated by Kristin Ross. Stanford, CA: Stanford University Press.
———. 2009. "A Few Remarks on the Method of Jacques Rancière." *Parallax* 15 (3): 114–23.

CHAPTER 10

Notes on The Poetics of Supervision

WHY WOULD ANYONE want to become a teacher? What at first glance feels like a test question will turn out to become a startling way to conceptualize the poetics of supervision. The nature of this creativity, however, involves interpreting conscious and unconscious obstacles and inhibitions in teacher education that confine both this question and the supervisor's work to the supposed realism of classroom observation. The wish to be watched and to watch will take us into a forgotten history of learning for love and having to grow up in the classrooms that one returns to as an adult. Bringing the past to bear upon the confines of the present will be one way to transform an understanding of experience in supervision into a philosophical problem of value and desire, akin to what the program of abstract art gives us over to think: an encounter with what is evocative in the assemblage of material, in lines of force and resistance, in the play of light and darkness, and in the fading away of objects. These dynamics belong to being in language, where the cast of a self's shadow falls into the epic of words. If the supervisory relationship can be imagined as an experiment in the field of speech, a new dialogue on the contentious problem of learning can be made from the vantage of listening to and elaborating the language of teaching. Then, when the subject represents her or his practices to another, supervision will find itself wandering into the thicket of what is most enigmatic in the desire to become a speaking subject.

Yet when asked why anyone would want to become a teacher, beginners repeat or feel that they must repeat stock answers to be intelligible to whomever they imagine the questioner to represent. Replies go something like this: I want to become a teacher because I care about children or love my subject area that has been ruined by others; I feel the call to be helpful to society and to the future; I wish to emulate a past teacher who helped me and be a role model to others who have none; I need to change the educational establishment because of my own (bad or good) experience as a student. Supervisors are rarely asked why they want to become a supervisor, although they, too, may say they supervise only to improve practices, share their experience, and help others avoid what has already happened to them. But this reduces everyone to needs waiting to be met, spoken about rather than urged to speak. It is as if, in the effort to firmly distinguish good from bad and success from failure, the profession must guarantee itself before the time of understanding. In other words, the profession is caught in the trap of repeating mantras of teaching without remembering or working through childhood phantasies, anxieties, and defenses made from being educated while educating others. The one question that can link teacher desire to her or his formation collapses under the weight of compliance with and anticipation of what one could or should say, only to indicate more about professional anxiety and the ego defenses of altruistic surrender and undoing what has already happened. So how might this question be used to understand the surprise of autonomy and the chance desire carries in becoming a teacher?

I turn to educational experiments in the training of the psychoanalyst, where practices, theories, and supervisions are the laboratory for the creation of the analyst's subjective position: her or his freedom to speak. I'll make a case for a comparable orientation for educators. I conclude with a short description from my work in public supervision with teachers in Istanbul. My argument is that attention to the formation of desire—or the signature of the teacher's original style and manner of work—can direct the institutions of teacher education and help us imagine the conditions that would allow for the courage to craft a subjective position in a profession. Such emotional work is dependent upon passing from being a student to the desire to take on the responsibilities of teaching.

A central discussion in the education of psychoanalysts concerns the idea that wanting to become a practitioner belongs to the work of assuming a subjective position within the responsibilities, doubts, questions, and creativity of a profession. From the beginning of Freud's discovery of the unconscious, education becomes both entangled in love and hate and in the vicissitudes of phantasy life and as a force that animates interest in creating something beyond what we feel we already know (Britzman 2009). Any education will suffer from this radical indeterminacy even as one may wish for coherence. And psychoanalytic supervision inherits and welcomes this dilemma. Contemporary literature on psychoanalytic supervisions resides in this scene, where the analyst, from the most to least experienced, presents his or her work to others for discussion and study. While there are significant differences in theoretical vantage across psychoanalytic schools of thought, and, too, a view that one's conceptual geography affects and may inhibit the generation of the meanings of practice, accounts of supervision have in common an endorsement of the ethics of open-mindedness, open discussion, respect for the unknown, and the interest in considering one's work from a new vantage (Levy 2007). Such aesthetic values place supervision in the paradox of transmitting the unknown and creating new knowledge that perhaps could not be seen during the time of practice.

Psychoanalytic supervision furthers the enigmas of practice by putting into words what is most difficult, courageous, and elusive in undergoing the work (Bion 2000, 2005a; Meltzer 2003; Rubinstein 2007). These published clinical supervisions, grounded in the enigmas of representing practice through speech and writing and so of having nothing less than the ambiguities of language to signify the afterwardness of meaning, invite and even call into being new paradoxes for the studio of supervision. They present the analytic function not so much in terms of what happened, or as information to receive and then reapply to others, but rather as occurring within supervision and so as requiring the containment of interpretation to evoke new questions, thus turning a case into a case study. For example, here is how Bion (2005a) began one of his supervisory seminars: "Does anyone feel the urge to express an idea or have an idea expressed?" (69). Immediately, someone asked a large question about the nature of time in psychoanalysis.

Bion then wondered what initiated the topic. In this supervision, Bion's work was to associate what went on behind the scenes by breathing life into the question, giving the question back, and permitting the questioner time to think. In Bion's (2005b) *The Tavistock Seminars*, things did not go as well. The editors of the recorded transcriptions noted a terrible heatwave and drought. The questions for Bion were inaudible; we only have his thoughts on who knows what, and finally, when the questions were audible, Bion's discussion ignored them. Quinodoz and colleagues (2006) have argued that the future of psychoanalysis depends upon the capacity to transmit with creativity, the lively nature of psychoanalytic experience. They ask, "How to transmit to a supervisee the audacity to be an analyst?" (342). They argue that the work of supervision occurs when the supervisee frees herself to express new questions.

The field of education does not have a comparable archive to enliven discussions on the clinical supervision of its practices. Indeed, our vocabulary confines supervision to the problem of beginners. The emphasis is on the immediacy of sight: the supervisor observes unfolding experience by privileging what is known as instruction on 'best practices.' The efforts of the one supervised is treated as if it is a behavioral problem of applying the stimulus of performance objectives to the engine of the student's learning, and outlining next steps. From either side of the divide, supervision is devoid of irony needed to engage in what is unknowable about our work as teachers. Compare this view with psychoanalytic discussions: the supervisor listens to the analyst's notes on and thoughts about a session that has already occurred, and so the supervisor occupies an ironic position within ignorance so as to teach this very stance of working from the unknown. The clinical event is gone so the presentation of clinical fragments—remnants in the form of a few sentences without the burden of a case history, or sometimes associated to with the help of passages from a novel, poem, or work of art that renders anew the aesthetic conflicts analysts undergo—extends the duration of practice with the work of clarifying thinking, engaging in private reverie, and even publicly dreaming. In the psychoanalytic literature on supervision, moving from one's personal analysis to the desire to become an analyst and assume the responsibilities of the analytic function is the central question.

The idea of a subjective position is developed in the seminars of Jacques Lacan. His seminars on teaching and learning are slowly entering the field of education with the work of educational theorists such as Felman (1987), Aoki (2000, 2002), Pitt (2003), Pinar (2004), Taubman (2006), and Silin (1995). These theorists note the complexity of Lacan's language and use his theories of language to enlarge discussion on the emotional landscape of education through the structural critique of our avoidances, blind spots, realism, and rationality. Rose (2000), however, has argued that one of the great repressions in North American discussions of Lacanian thought concern the dearth of examining his interest in the training of analysts as the key psychoanalytic problematic animating his theory.

From 1953 to 1980, Lacan held 27 yearly seminars, at least six of which have been published and translated into English; while the majority is unpublished and circulate in pirated form. Analysts, candidates in training, teachers, graduate students, the public, and French intellectuals from fields such as mathematics, social thought, linguistics, anthropology, and philosophy attended his seminars. While Lacan's views are used today in a range of academic discussions to think about the subject and its formation in the registers of the real, the imaginary, and the symbolic, his attention to teaching, learning, and the question of the analyst's education throughout these seminars is not well known. The time has come, Rose argued, to use Lacan to wonder what is wrong with our educational institutions from their inside. And this entails, Rose (2000) suggests, raising a fundamental question, one I use to structure my understanding of supervision:

> Why would anyone want to become an analyst? You might ask in reply: Why does anyone ever want to become anything at all? But in relation to psychoanalysis, the question has particular resonance, since it is a central part of psychoanalysis to ask how you come to recognize and misrecognise yourself in what you are. And since behind, or inside, that question will be the question of desire—the aims, vicissitudes and perversions of our pleasures—'wanting', no less than 'becoming', is something you cannot take for granted . . . it can only be the start. (25)

I am proposing that desire—the subject's ardor and passion of wanting to become something more for its own sake—is risked in the decision to become a teacher. But this then means that one's motives and interests play between the poles of recognition and misrecognition since not only does the teacher desire the recognition of others in the performative space of teaching but if one is to continue doing such work, one must also wonder how this desire becomes transformed by the other in one's practices.

My modest contribution, then, focuses on a few of Lacan's comments on supervision that he tied to the formation of the psychoanalyst, with the idea that a second look at the conflicts in the education of psychoanalysts—of moving from being a patient to wanting to assume the position of the analyst—may lend teacher education new terms for imagining supervision as one of the key conditions for inviting the desire to move from the position of the student to assuming the subjective position of teacher. This direction involves, as we shall see, the supervisor's suspension of certainty seemingly made from classroom observation for the desire of the work of speech in formulating one's understanding of the desire to teach. What if teaching, and our reflection on it, takes us not to the undoing of classroom reality, itself the ambiguous, fleeting context of the teacher's work, but rather takes its force from the limits and pleasures of representing the teacher's learning? What if we think of supervision as a transitional space made from opening new dimensions of experience unavailable at the time of its unfolding?

Two metaphors, borrowed from art and psychoanalysis, can extend the situation of the teacher's education: supervision as poetics, or a style of listening that draws attention to the literary dimensions of the limit of experience from the vantage of its gaps, silences, edges, and condensations, and supervision as akin to thought experiments, a clinical description

Freud ([1911] 1966) used to describe the work of thinking and imagination, constructions that need not rely on reality as a standard of affectivity and constraint. Both metaphors bring us to the symbolic register and pose new problems in the work of getting to know reality and phantasy. Whereas the first metaphor carries traces of philosophical discussions of modernism in art, the second proposes thinking as an experimental form of action and invites the psychoanalytic problem of desire and misrecognition.

Poetics, as a theoretical approach to the literary stylistics and architecture of language, now extends from the field of poetry to contemporary discussions on aesthetics. Gianni Vattimo (2008), for example, proposes that from the perspective of art, the twentieth century can be characterized as one of poetics, a century preoccupied with the values of representing the aesthetics of experience from within the pressure of post positivistic philosophical assertions that the foundation of knowledge has no ultimate cause or originary moment. The program of meaning is always being written and revised. The temporality of poetics therefore speaks not to what has already occurred but rather with potential. In this view, there is no pure essence, no reality to be secured and repeated through the problem of representing experience, no ultimate transcendence made from the capture of observation, and no safe passage that opens direct access to pure meaning. Essentially, as a theory of textuality, the poetics of representation links the creation of meaning to the problem of signifiers, interpretation, and truth effects. Attention to the poetics of experience carries new dilemmas for the understanding the play of authentication, evidence, and validity.

The second metaphor for supervision leans on the imaginative mode of the *as if*, a suspension of action that Freud ([1911] 1966) called thinking. This temporality is one of deferral, in the sense that thinking gathers up the threads of frustration and is the means for understanding the afterwardness of doing or action. Freud argued that thinking is an emotional achievement of the psychical mind. Our earliest inclination toward the reduction of frustration is to hallucinate satisfaction, to scream and cry, then try to change the environment through bodily action, and, finally, to think about frustration which involves holding what is undesirable in the mind, even if it does not alter the actual frustration. Because one holds in the mind the idea of event and the affects associated with the event, thinking is never so far away from wishing for a new world and creating new elements for the imagination.

Supervision As The Given And The Possible

For some time, I have been thinking about supervision as a work of language: as a dialogue made from the exchange of words on the nature, tension, surprise, anxiety, and mishap of interpreting the constructions of practice and as effecting the practitioner's transformation. It can be a thinking scene where the mind is made up, not from the vantage of certitude but from new forms of mindfulness to what becomes of desire for the work.

This orientation emerges from my psychoanalytic training where I experienced supervision and my work as a supervisor in the context of the university. I believe that in both contexts, practice and its supervision always involve fiddling with three dimensions of experiencing experience that compose shared problems between supervisor and supervisee, between teacher and student, and between analyst and patient.

The first is the manifest dimension of experience. It feels idiomatic, in the sense of its immediacy or what, in the education field, is thought of as thinking on one's feet: feeling the force of situations without the benefit of second thoughts or the capacity to slow down the event to consider what could not be known at the time but nonetheless leaves one with the excess of affect. In the manifest dimension, one does not know the consequences of one's actions or how others might perceive and feel the unfolding events. One may not even really know how one feels at the time of the event's unfolding. This first dimension is best thought of as standing experience: tolerating having to act before one knows, and therefore working from ignorance, and as being able to stand the force of experience that does structure one's teaching acts.

The second dimension of experience begins with these blind spots, how not seeing animates intention, misses its gratification, and fades into the twilight of events. The turn is to speak from the exigencies of what practice has had to defer in order to practice at all. One might then wonder what else one might now think and try to understand the reasoning behind one's actions, not from the automation of stimulus and response but more abstractly, from a theoretical vantage of the action's phenomenology. The third dimension concerns the dream work of supervision, itself an experience of free-floating attention to the procedures of the mind that creates the ways in which narration of the events migrates to the day's residues and where the object of desire becomes more abstract, overdetermined, and more affecting. Supervision, then, is dialogue that moves from the surface of experience to its depth psychology and then backs over the event, prolonging its duration, expanding experience with its lines of flight, force, and areas of confusion and fusion. All these emotional shadings are met by irony. After all, the event is already gone even if it can be felt once again.

The large problem for teacher education is whether supervision can stop fixating on urgent experience. In the initial teacher education, supervision occurs before the supervisor—known in the research literature as 'the significant other' and known by the student teacher as 'the big other'—enters the student teacher's classroom world and seems to actualize it (Britzman 2003). Yet even before this event, there stands a phantasy of the supervisor. The ritual of supervision, which takes place in school settings, sustains the phantasy of the supervisor as omnipotent and so as subject-presumed-to-know. Whether the supervisor appears unannounced or tediously schedules her visit in advance, on this special day the student teacher is, to say the least, quite nervous, more student, less teacher. These events have an afterlife in memory's anticipations: the imaginary supervisor represents a judge of events, an anticipator of teaching accidents, and a finger-wagger of boundary crossings. Some supervisors believe it is a good idea to serve as the student teacher's auxiliary superego. Others feel that the supervisor in the student teacher's mind functions to diminish or inhibit imagination, somehow pulling the strings of the student teacher's own judgment, confining her to the lowest denominator of adaptation to prevailing safe practices. The phantasy of the supervisor as commanding figure demands that one follow a plan, know in advance what is correct and incorrect, or good or bad, and maintain a schizoid attitude toward practice. Gray areas are to be either avoided or corrected, and so the problem of compliance, an obstacle to desire, is not linked to the supervisor's classroom presence. Thus, our implication in how we sustain dependency and helplessness is hardly considered and this makes it nearly impossible to critique our own hand in objectification and domination.

What is it like to be observed? I have heard student teachers speak of their supervision as "being on Broadway." They believe they must be upbeat, in control, and enthusiastic, all at the same time, and performing this excited show of affect will somehow telegraph to the audience supervisor their commitment to be an upbeat teacher. The student teacher must not be depressed. They may prepare their classroom students in advance with a secret pact by asking them to behave and to be upbeat when the supervisor comes to evaluate. Student teachers are worried that the supervisor can see through them and so record each and every mistake and achievement to be used either to ruin a fledgling career or applaud the victorious, perfect lesson. Both measures of success and failure take the form of projective identifications: anxiety is projected into the supervisor, who is then identified with since what is actually projected are parts of the student teacher's self. While this phantasy raises the question of who is watching whom, it also works to destroy thinking.

Once the lesson is completed the student teacher and the supervisor sit together and go over the immediate events, usually from the vantage of matching the supervisor's observations to the student teacher's teaching objectives. This exercise is repeated throughout the student teacher's university education. It is also dreaded and disclaimed and, for both parties, serves as a source of frustration and a repetition of the immediacy of an overwhelming experience. Even when supervision is posed as collaboration or as a helping relationship, even when its theories are drawn from the designs of clinical supervision, discussion tends to revolve around the lesson's effectiveness, itself defined by way of maintaining behavioral objectives, curricular goals, and the strength of the lesson plan. In all these events, supervision sustains the phantasy that there can be a supposed and planned reality that nonetheless leaves in its wake planted evidence of incompetence or success. If we do understand that reality cannot be planned, that it exits without us, that areas of confusion and accidents conflict within the narcissism of intentions, and that there is far more to reality than we can see at any time, our dominant model of supervision forecloses unknown reality by privileging, with the failed guarantee, the phantasy that seeing is believing and that reality matches implementation.

So much is missed in all of this anxiety. But even more, anxiety is made, now from the vantage of the supervisor, when she or he is asked to imagine supervision without the classroom observation and as consisting as a speech act made from the candidate's presentation of her or his work. Many of my university colleagues in teacher education, for example, feel that their own effectiveness would be compromised if they could not see what is going on in the student teacher's classroom. They worry the student teacher might lie to them and only present the good fictive moments or, even worse, make up their entire classroom experience in order to pass. They worry that without seeing classroom students and the student teacher's interactions with them, they would have only half of the picture. They wonder about what would constitute evidence of effectiveness if there were only words. For the supervisor, then, there is a great deal of anxiety about her or his own subjective position when he or she tries to imagine working from ignorance. And certainly, this conceptual frame of supervision as a speech act urges a new subjective position for everyone, becoming a problem of poetics, more like encountering abstract art, an adventure in constructing enigmas, including a different understanding of what may agitate and animate value and desire. When listening to the material of signifiers, supervision as a speech act does become dreamier, more ironic when one bumps into the ambiguity of experience, and more uncertain when experience is presented in its many conflictive dimensions. Indeed, supervision becomes just like the performativity of teaching and learning.

Lacan's Experiment

After breaking from the French branch of the International Psychoanalytic Association, Lacan gave what has come to be known as "The Rome Address" to the 1953 Conference of Psychoanalysts of the Romance Languages (Roudinesco 1990). The paper ran about 150 pages, and Lacan spoke from his major points, launching a scathing critique of the psychoanalytic establishment from the vantage of its training procedures and constraints. He argued that as practice, theory, and event, psychoanalysis has yet to psychoanalyze itself with the consequence of retreating from Freud's radical discovery. In what now reads as a most baroque eulogy, peppered with accusations of idiocy, jokes, and puns of language, his key insistence was with the creativity of speech: that first and foremost, psychoanalysis is made from speech acts only for the purpose of providing a chance for the speaking subject to assume a new subjective position in desire. This Lacan ([1953] 2006) called "the gift of speech" (265): that in putting things into words, speech inaugurates the subject as an agent of language, as speaking rather than as spoken, even as this speech says more than it can mean because of the poetic properties of language as such. Lacan demonstrated this paradox through his critique of the psychoanalyst's problem of education, training, and supervision. Ten years later, "The Rome Address" would eventually lead to the establishment of his own school, Ecole Freudienne de Paris. The school did not last long, and Safouan (2000) noted the need to study it as an exemplary experiment in failure.

There are many ways to tell this story of the internecine battle between schools of thought; this was neither the first fight in the psychoanalytic field nor its last. And these controversies, if they are to be understood as a cul-de-sac in thinking, can instruct the problem of what resists assuming the risks of innovation. In her discussion of Lacan's long career as a founder of his own school of psychoanalysis, Roudinesco (1990) posits a constitutive paradox of every psychoanalytic society and that can be extended to any educational institution:

> The history of psychoanalytic societies reveals something unprecedented: The more one favors the emergence of a democratic power founded on a respect for the ideas of individuals, the more one tends to eradicate the work of the unconscious. One ends up supporting a guarantee for the ego, that is, an associative guild mentality, to the detriment of a theoretical struggle intent on decentering the position of the subject. (224)

While it is beyond the scope of this chapter to detail the many missteps and ultimate collapse of Lacan's school and his part in that, Roudinesco suggests we pay close attention to how our goals become confused with desire and what happens to us when educational experimentation works as an internal critique of its instituted program. Can any institution sustain perpetual disruptions without calling upon its need for stability, recognition, and indelibility? And what happens to that other disruption, the eruptions of unconscious, that carry the affected ego beyond its own designs and into what it does not know?

Lacan's "Rome Address" placed the function of speech at the heart of becoming a subject. He claimed that experience—whether in clinical practice or life itself—is neither didactic nor instructive, and as a way to consider the designs of speech, he even joked that the best preparation for the analyst was to practice doing crossword puzzles, for there, with only clues, one plays with the allusions of language and the ambiguity of the signifier, thus entering into the problem of referentiality from the vantage position of the ironic stretch of meaning and the work of associating with signs. He situated the psychoanalytic dilemma of education in the problem of speech, of having something to say that sets in motion both a desire for recognition and the problem of addressing the other. In his "Rome Address," Lacan ([1953] 2006) wrote that psychoanalytic experience "exploits the poetic function of language to give [human] desire its symbolic mediation" (264).

By 1963 Lacan launched a new Freudian school with the purpose of redesigning the nature of the analyst's education, heightening the problem of assuming the analyst's position, and removing education from the hierarchy of psychoanalytic institutes. He placed the problem of becoming an analyst in the analyst's hands. The issue was not to apply technique, but to think through the technical as a portal into the existential problems of knowledge, authority, and hierarchy that, from the beginning of psychoanalysis, has plagued and inhibited psychoanalytic institutes. Lacan's declaration was stark: "The analyst's authorization derives from her-or himself alone" (as cited in Rose 2000, 6). This is an audacious pass for any education. It also presents the question of becoming an analyst as the desire to be a speaking subject able to stand the many conflictive, idiomatic, and surprising dimensions of experience.

Lacan's school was based on the supposition that both teachers and candidates would, by necessity and structure, be in relation to the testimony of the candidate's desire to move from the subjective position of the analysand, or the experience of undergoing her or his personal analysis, to that of becoming an analyst interested in analyzing others. Here is where we can draw a parallel to the teacher's world: after years of being a student and growing up in a place called school, the student may desire to take on the teacher's position. What is this desire? Here is the crossroad where the experience of education transforms from something one undergoes to something one desires to direct. Safouan's (2000) discussion of Lacan's educational experiment posed the school's problem as "how to understand the project of someone seeking to become an analyst" (104–5). This principle of autonomy then required the school to bear witness to the candidate's testimony of learning. The guarantee of practice, however, must belong to the new analyst and not to the school, which can only testify when the exercise could be over. Much was unknown, as Lacan ([1953] 2006) admitted, and he drew a parallel to the duration of analysis "based on the limits of our field . . . we cannot predict how long a subject's time for understanding will last, insofar as it includes a psychological factor that escapes us by its very nature" (255). The gap of education would be made from the distance between the time of understanding and the moment of conclusion. It would be the candidate's responsibility to grapple with these differential dimensions of experience and put them into speech.

Lacan's ([1953] 2006) discussion of supervision emerges from his critique of psychoanalysis and his understanding that psychoanalytic treatment has at stake the status of desire, itself the signifying function of the symbolic and the means for the subject to emerge from objectification. It may seem odd that Lacan had to argue for the value and ambiguities of speech in a field that is known as "the talking cure," but one of the large problems Lacan addressed was how, in the name of developmental correction, psychoanalysts mistook the patient's demands for unmet needs and, in so doing, forgot how their own need to help affects the analytic function. Needs, he implied, took psychoanalysis back to biology, whereas demands placed the analysis in the speech act and brought to the fore paradoxes of recognition, desire, and truth. In psychoanalytic treatment, it is not the patient's reality that is addressed but rather the way the patient speaks from her world, signifying a desire for that world. When the analyst seeks supervision for a case, the same process is repeated: the supervisor depends only upon listening to the analyst's speech. Actual contact with the analyst and patient's reality is prohibited. "The very possibility of that supervision," wrote Lacan "would become problematic from the perspective of contact with the patient's reality [*réel*]. On the contrary, the supervisor manifests a second sight—that's the world for it!—which makes the experience at least as instructive for him as for his supervisee" (210).

And so the analyst refracts the patient's discourse and in doing so affects her own speech. Supervision resides in this process as well and the supervisor is changed, only supervising to experiment with ideas, listen to the work of others, and grapple again with technical concepts for the purpose of creating a style of work. To bring poetics to the fore Lacan likened the soundings of supervision to the musician's transformation of a musical score: the notes are not merely read and reproduced without difference, but because of the musician's interpretive signature, new variations of meaning can be played and heard. In supervision, the analyst's notes are taken through the many dimensions experience invokes. The supervisor is like an echo:

> If the supervisee could be put by the supervisor into a subjective position different from that implied by the sinister term *contrôle* (advantageously replaced, but only in English, by "supervision"), the greatest benefit he would derive from this exercise would be to learn to put himself in the position of that second subjectivity into which the situation automatically puts the supervisor. (Lacan [1953] 2006, 210)

In the supervisory relation, both parties work from their desire for a new subjective position.

Near the end of his "Rome Address," Lacan ([1953] 2006) pressured the work of the teacher in these terms:

> I consider it to be an urgent task to disengage from concepts that are being deadened by routine use, the meaning they recover when we reexamine their history and reflect on their subjective foundations.
>
> That, no doubt, is the teacher's prime function—the function on which all the others depend—and the one in which the value of experience figures best. (199–200)

Desire In Teacher Education

I would like to extend my observations on psychoanalytic education into the field of teacher education with an example of public supervision held for educators, social workers, graduate students, nongovernmental organization workers, psychoanalysts, and the general public. In the winter of 2007, I was invited to an education and psychoanalysis conference titled "Re-imagining Education" held in the MEF School in Istanbul, Turkey. Along with giving a talk that was translated into Turkish and French, I was asked to conduct a two-hour public supervision workshop. I questioned what, if anything, I had to offer Turkish teachers and while at first, I worried how the translation of my words from

English to French and to Turkish would affect the fragility of communication, second thoughts led me to wonder about my own fragility in such work.

Prior to attending the conference, I received a case report that involved a foreign language teacher of English and her breakdown with a bilingual child, a boy of about seven years old, whose parents moved from Turkey to Germany to attend graduate school and then, about five years later, the family returned to Turkey for their profession. Upon arriving at the new school, the little boy refused to learn or speak in her class. He followed no directions, and the teacher would often find herself yelling at the child and then sending him off to the principal's office. I recall, when trying to prepare, a feeling that I must be missing a page of the report, that I had lost key details, along with any clarity as to what drama occurred for the many actors involved. I felt I had received the bare outlines and then wondered how this case would turn into a case study. This report raised a number of questions, the foremost one being, What is the desire of the child student and the teacher in this language class? Much later, near the end of our supervision workshop, we transformed this question into, What is our desire as we interpret this long-gone event?

I began this work of supervision with a strong dose of ignorance as to this Turkish school's actual working conditions and knew nothing about their professional culture, conflicts, and desires in education. The case was read to the audience, now through the tonality, rhythms, and sounds of Turkish and French. As words I could not understand wafted throughout the room, I wondered what the audience heard. What words caught them? I also wondered, as the translator whispered English into my ear, what I was hearing. I only had the good sense to speak slowly, and my first comment was that before we could begin to discuss what we heard, we would all have to become lost in translation. All of us were working from our ignorance and our capacity to stand that experience. That was my comment to them and from there we found ourselves trying out our respective desires for education, slowly turning the case into a case study of our desires.

A lively discussion ensued, carried by the teachers' investments, phantasies, and anxieties with cultural differences in school; the parent's role in the child's school refusal; the teacher's insensitivity to the child; the child's motivations and feelings; and the school administration's means of addressing whatever problem they could grasp. I began to realize that all of us were dreaming up the teacher, the parent, and the child from the vantage of what we imagined language meant for them, how it came to be that the child's silence invoked the teacher's yelling, and whether the child was ingenious in finding a way to leave a class. This level of overwhelming experience gave us access to our emotional investments in needing to secure a reality we did not know. There was a wish for a coherent story, even as we had received a story of breakdown. What required clarification was how we listened, and only then could discussion turn to what we imagined as the problem, how our areas of confusion stretched our phantasies of education.

I questioned our investments in an education without conflict and acknowledged the poetic fact that despite our feelings of urgency—an indicator of the transference—we were interpreting a text. The stakes began with signifying our approaches to what we imagined happened and what this suggests about our educational desires. This limit slowed down the need to fix something and led to speculation on how we were affected by what we could not know. I noticed that the ways in which some teachers in the audience described the child's dilemma signified something more to explore about our situation: that when we imagine education, we may be both eluding and signifying our desire.

Reality was elusive, then, and now, the transference was alive, the conflicts were circulating, and all we could do was challenge ourselves to interpret the contours of our own phantasies, using these wishes and anxieties as resources for thinking from the subjective position of ourselves as teachers. We were now engaged in multiple dimensions of experience, analyzing our urgency, blind spots, and our interest in what our depictions of the teacher and student signified for our thinking. Gradually the supervision grew more abstract and was used to articulate a range of ideas under the theme of problems of knowing, being, and doing, all of which constitute the teacher's desire for work and the vulnerability made when we realized that the paper teacher and child were our screen upon which we projected our anxieties, expelling this danger onto a failed teacher or child and giving up a chance to ask, Why would anyone want to become a teacher? We were also close to the impossible question, Why would anyone want to be a child? The supervision moved from the question of what was the problem of the other to what problems do we have in understanding.

I provide this example as punctuation to illustrate how supervision, as a field of speech, enacts new subjective positions. After the events of teaching, the work continues, now in the abstract domain of understanding the play of signifiers. What lingers on and requires analysis is the teacher's desire to take on this new subjective position, one dependent upon a field of speech and the poetics of learning to listen. This is the supervisor's case as well.

Bibliography

Aoki, Douglas Sadao. 2000. "The Thing Never Speaks for Itself: Lacan and the Politics of Clarity." *Harvard Educational Review* 70 (3): 347–69.

———. 2002. "The Price of Teaching: Love, Evasion and the Subordination of Knowledge." *JCT: Journal of Curriculum Theorizing* 18 (1): 21–39.

Bion, Wilfred R. 2000. *Clinical Seminars and Other Works*. Edited by Francesca Bion. London: Karnac Books.

———. 2005a. *The Italian Seminars*. Translated by Philip Slotkin. London: Karnac Books.

———. 2005b. *The Tavistock Seminars*. Edited by Francesca Bion. London: Karnac Books.

Britzman, Deborah P. 2003. *Practice Makes Practice: A Critical Study of Learning to Teach*. Revised edition. Albany: State University of New York Press.

———. 2009. *The Very Thought of Education: Psychoanalysis and the Impossible Professions*. Albany: State Univeristy of New York Press.

Felman, Shoshana. 1987. *Jacques Lacan and the Adventure of Insight: Psychoanalysis in Contemporary Culture*. Cambridge, MA: Harvard University Press.

Freud, Sigmund. (1911) 1966. "Formulation of Two Principles of Mental Functioning." In *The Standard Edition of the Complete Psychological Works of Sigmund Freud, Volume XII (1911–1913): The Case of Schreber, Papers on Technique and Other Works*, edited and translated by James Strachey, in collaboration with Anna Freud, 215–26. London: Hogarth Press.

Lacan, Jacques. (1953) 2006. "The Function and Field of Speech and Language in Psychoanalysis." In *Écrits.: The First Complete Edition in English*, translated by Bruce Fink, in collaboration with Héloïse Fink and Russell Grigg, 197–268. New York: W. W. Norton & Company.

Levy, Joshua. 2007. "Commentary." In *Talking about Supervision: 10 Questions, 10 Analysts=100 Answers*, edited by Laura Elliot Rubinstein, 107–20. London: International Psychoanalytical Association.

Meltzer, Donald, with Rosa Castellà, Carlos Tabbia, and Lluís Farré. 2003. *Supervisions with Donald Meltzer*. London: Karnac Books.

Pinar, William, F. 2004. *What is Curriculum Theory?* Mahwah, NJ: Lawrence Erlbaum Associates, Inc.

Pitt, Alice. 2003. *The Play of the Personal: Psychoanalytic Narratives of Feminist Education*. New York: Peter Lang Press.

Quinodoz, Danielle, Aubry, Candy, Bonard, Olivier, Déjussel, Geneviève, and Bernard Reith. 2006. "Being a Psychoanalyst: An Everyday Audacity." Translated by David Alcorn. *International Journal of Psychoanalysis* 87 (2): 329–47.

Rose, Jacqueline. 2000. "Introduction." In *Jacques Lacan and the Question of Psychoanalytic Training* by Moustapha Safouan, translated by Jacqueline Rose, 1–48. New York: St. Martin's Press.

Roudinesco, Elizabeth. 1990. *Jacques Lacan & Co.: A History of Psychoanalysis in France, 1925–1985*. Translated by Jeffrey Mehlman. Chicago: University of Chicago Press.

Rubinstein, Laura Elliot, ed. 2007. *Talking about Supervision: 10 Questions, 10 Analysts=100 Answers*. London: International Psychoanalytical Association.

Safouan. Moustapha. 2000. *Jacques Lacan and the Question of Psychoanalytic Training*. Translated by Jacqueline Rose. New York: St. Martin's Press.

Silin, Jonathan. 1995. *Sex, Death, and the Education of Children: Our Passion for Ignorance in the Age of AIDS*. New York: Teacher's College Press.

Taubman, Peter. 2006. "I Love Them to Death." In *On the Return of Love and Childhood: Psychoanalytic Theory in Teaching and Learning*, edited by Gail M. Boldt and Paula M. Salvio, 19–32. New York: Routledge Press.

Vattimo, Gianni. 2008. *Art's Claim to Truth*. Translated by Luca D'Isanto. New York: Columbia University Press.

CHAPTER 11

Some Psychoanalytic Observations On Ordinary, Quiet, And Painful Resistance

To be completely honest with oneself is a good practice.
—SIGMUND FREUD, LETTER TO FLIESS, 1897

MY DISCUSSION LOOKS into the work of learning in the overabundant studio of resistance. I take an ironic position in that I am trying to grasp what is ineffable, uncertain, easily missed, and quite ordinary. With psychoanalysis, I address a few problems made in educational contexts when trying to translate beleaguered resistance into a vocabulary of psychological significance. This vocabulary, too, is easily lost or diminished, since all at once resistance indexes painful conflicts of meaning, self/other relations, and desire. Taken to their heights in education such conflicts present intimate dilemmas within authorship, responsibility, and intersubjectivity. Can our practices and theories of teaching and learning be instructed by the twists and turns of resistance? What can educators learn from the part they play in the theatre of resistance to learning?

To enter this internal world is painful; there are worries over what may be lost and found and, too, astounding questions. What is being asked of me? What do I want? How do I contain incompatible ideas, say those that defy consciousness, ordinary modes of thought, and social conventions? All this requires an open mind, a challenge made even more complicated since, as the great irony psychoanalysis teaches, exploring the unconscious is itself subject to resistance. And this leaves the question: Who resists?

Education is no stranger to resistance but to understand resistance with irony requires the guidance of philosophy, literature, and psychoanalysis. Kierkegaard ([1861] 1989) places the concept of irony within the pedagogical action urged in Socratic dialogue. So many of Socrates's teaching questions begin by asking what cannot be answered, such as what is the nature of love, knowledge, and virtue and how or whether they can be taught and learned. The ironic Socrates was most interested in ignorance and the ways of hubris, all qualities of experience we wish to know nothing about. Kierkegaard pushes these ideas further when he points to subjectivity with the suggestion that we humans are figures of speech. "Irony," Kierkegaard wrote, "is a qualification of subjectivity" (262). It divides subjectivity, making it less absolute, less unified, and more vulnerable to its own desire. The most ironic qualification is that the human is subject to symbolization and responsible for self-understanding. While humans can never be free of history, accidents, and chance, with irony one can enter a field of possibilities. Irony holds in store pedagogical action, a transformation of knowledge and the self.

Psychoanalysis enters with the claim that an awareness of irony facilitates new styles of emotional freedom and therapeutic action. Jonathan Lear's (2003) discussion of therapeutic action makes an eloquent argument for psychoanalytic irony as an invitation to communication that includes discussion of the problem of inhibition, or what stops narrative freedom. So, the work itself is subject to critique. It all hinges on the handling of resistance. I hope to show how, from the side of ordinary, painful, and quiet resistance, we can listen to desire and transform the ways in which we respond to its many objections.

A Brief History of Freud's Learning

Freud began with a study of his own resistance. It came in the form of writing blocks, self-disappointment, and general malaise. In 1897, he wrote to Wilhelm Fliess of his breakthrough:

> To be completely honest with oneself is good practice. One single thought of general value has been revealed to me. I have found in my own case, too, falling in love with the mother and jealously of the father, and I now regard it as a universal event of early childhood.... If that is so, we can understand the riveting power of Oedipus Rex, in spite of all the objections raised by reason against its presupposition of destiny; and we can understand why the later 'dramas of destiny' were bound to fail so miserably. Our feelings rise against any arbitrary individual compulsion.... But the Greek legend seizes on a compulsion which everyone recognizes because he feels its existence within himself. Each member of the audience was once, in germ and in phantasy, just such an Oedipus, and each one recoils in horror from the dream-fulfillment here transplanted into reality, with the whole quota of repression which separate his infantile state from his present one. (265)

In one fell swoop, we meet the discovery of psychoanalysis and resistance to it. After all, one of the most original claims Freud made is that the child's libidinal relations to her or his parents are the transit visas for subjectivity, sexuality, and intersubjectivity. There is a great deal to resist in Freud's insistence, even as he proposes what we already may know: that the impressionable, dependent human is an erotic creature. We are inaugurated by love, convinced by phantasy, and riveted by desire. Freud, too, finds something affecting within the Oedipal drama—an incitement of hostility, jealously, sexuality, and interest. And these are the affective qualifications that compose one of the most difficult, endearing, and elemental educations we undergo, defend against, and try to forget.

But notice that Freud is speaking about desire just as much as resistance to it. Impressive phantasy life qualifies Freud to create theory. And it does for us all. What saves us from useless haphazardness and from the implosive repetition of long-ago events that seem to resist language is that we can put these feelings into words and learn more about our history of love and hate. With Freud's early comments on Oedipal conflicts, we can begin to think about why resistance is so difficult to symbolize. Its roots are deep, and its flowering tells an incredible story of our history of love and its dispersal into wishes, anxiety, phantasy, and defense.

From the beginning of his research, Freud understood desire as residing in such ordinary resistance as jokes, dreams, memory, slips of the tongue, and bungled actions. Here, ordinary resistance plays in the field of conscious intentions and unconscious wishes. But in his clinic, Freud began to think about the patient's resistance to his interpretations of symptoms of suffering. In the studio of overabundant resistance, Freud learned that simply telling patients about the meanings of their illness did not bring change. In the emotional world, our passionate convictions, what Kristeva (2009) has named "our incredible need to believe," are more convincing.

These objections led Freud to explore the gap between the analyst's interpretation of symptoms and the patient's acceptance of new meanings. Learning, Freud came to find, proceeds through breakdowns, resistance, and desire. Constructing meaning from this mismatch is what Freud (1914) called "working through." Freud preserved the idea that what is most meaningless holds meaning in store and his method of free association, of saying whatever comes to mind without censoring what is incompatible to ordinary modes of thought, is testimony to this first principle of psychoanalysis. Free speech or putting things into words also led to new forms of resistance and to Freud's rethinking of psychoanalytic technique and how resistance could even be approached. Eventually, he thought of resistance as the ego's objection, one of its many defenses against both the internal pressures of the id and the superego and the demands of the outside world. But this complexity of where danger resides meant that he had to keep open the questions of who resists and who constructs the path of least resistance.

Our Emotional Situation

While Freud's clinic played in the field of objections, his daughter, Anna Freud ([1930] 1974), brought psychoanalytic objections to education. She describes the situation with irony: education is defined as all types of interference. Even as we may know from noisy experience that teaching and learning are emotional situations, thinking about education as interference jars our sensibilities. We may scramble to protect our idealizations, think that only other people interfere but not ourselves, or wonder about our own clamors, times when interference was felt as either too much or not enough. Anna Freud, too, took the path of least resistance when she asked that in imagining education as all types of interference, we soften our resistances. Her last lecture began with this caution: "We must not demand too much from one another" (A. Freud [1930] 1974, 121).

Anna Freud seems to be speaking about two kinds of demands. There is the demand for the speaker to just get to the point and assure the audience that meaning is stable and easily digested. With her lecture she felt there was only so much that could be learned: some of her shortcuts could cause confusion, and psychoanalysis, her topic, carried more intricacies than she could convey. Alongside these reasons, she understood that learning demands set in motion a new resistance. Once problems are suggested, we want to solve them quickly and rush to prevention. But she also imagined a question her formulation raised:

> To know whether we, as adults, should interfere more or be less authoritarian than adults have in the past. In answer . . . I have to say that psychoanalysis so far has stood for limiting the efforts of education by emphasizing some specific dangers connected with it. (A. Freud [1930] 1974, 123)

This advice, too, may come as a surprise. Generally speaking, we may believe people need more education, not less. While Miss Freud was mainly thinking about authoritarian power—the ways, say, education presses the learner down, doles out punishments, and wishes to control students—if we take into account the tenderness of emotional life, there is a reason to limit the interference of sadistic power. But Miss Freud also gives another reason for thinking about education through its dangers. It has to do with the relation between education and the superego. The superego is an area of the psyche that is perhaps the harshest in demands. In classical Freudian terms, it is a remnant of Oedipal desires but now in the form of introjections of prohibitions. The superego is our internal judge and the command goes something like this: 'Be like me, you cannot be like me.' In this internalized court, where all roads lead to guilt, the ego never measures up. Even having to learn can be felt as needing to be punished. In this view, resistance is an internal affair. And it is the autobiography of learning that requires limits.

The specific dangers are made from learning relationships that simultaneously form the internal world and our anticipation for recognition from the external world of others. There is always the challenge of creating psychological meaning from what does feel like an overwhelming experience. And symbolizing impressive emotional life as formative to the self, knowledge, and others is as difficult to convey, as it is to tolerate and work from. Putting words to unaccountable feelings does mean thinking about emotional pain. And we may likely protect ourselves. Yet, while there is no escaping our emotional world, the largest danger in education is that more often than not, the emotional world of teaching and learning is left to languish in our private doubts. This is a more insidious form of resistance, for it leads to self-blame. If these feelings lag behind, we also manage to project them forward to forecast our fears, anxieties, and wishes.

Fragments Of Resistance

Imagine if these doubts could be spoken to others and heard as desire. What would they have to say and how would our listening be affected?

Here are four scripts, all fragments of quiet, ordinary, and painful resistance. They are not really dreams, but I will treat them as such. They all convey an uncanny estrangement and timelessness. Like dreams, they have an unfinished feel, as if important details have fallen away. For now, let them serve as our dream furniture.

1. An undergraduate university student who is studying teaching missed the deadline for handing in her final paper. A few days after the paper was due, she writes me a message filled with emergencies. A relative died, and then, just as she was about to write the paper, she had some kidney stones she needed to pass. She needs an extension and hopes she will not be punished. Six weeks later, she hands her late paper over to me. She writes about her disagreement with telling lies and berates problem children who cannot tell the truth because their family has taught them to lie to their unbelieving teachers.

2. A graduate student cannot hand in his paper. He sends me long written messages about not being able to write, that he has fallen into some personal difficulties and is trying to sort them out, and that he is deeply disappointed in not being able to write. When he begins to write, he hates what his paper cannot say. It isn't right, and he does not want to hand me the wrong paper. After handing in this paper, I receive a message from him. A mistake has been made and he handed in the wrong one. The paper was incomplete. Could he hand in a new one?

3. A patient has not been able to finish writing her research thesis. Years go by. Whenever she sits down to write, she has the sudden feeling that she must stop writing and run to the library to read more. She worries that her ideas are too late, that others have already written them down, and if this is so, then she might be accused of plagiarizing the work of others without even knowing she is doing so. The thesis has the feel of an accident or crime scene. But the clues do not add up.

4. A colleague worries she is a bad professor. She hates grading her students' papers and worries that with any grade she gives, she will either be accused of being unfair or too easy on the students' assignments. Both good and bad grades feel more like compliance with someone else's demands. She spends more and more time preparing for classes but feels unready. She anticipates her students' unanswerable questions as if they are testing her knowledge. She gives herself failing marks.

It is difficult to say what is being resisted and what is desired in these quiet, ordinary, and painful events. As guilty narratives of blame and fault, they implicate the listener and may also call forth resistance to hearing them. We may want to give advice, solve them quickly, take cover in institutional rules, and forget the educational dangers they signal. They may even call us to harsh action. After all, why should the teacher accept late papers? Why puzzle over the incomplete thought? Why wait for learning? Shouldn't we be teaching a lesson here? In the court of ordinary, quiet, and painful resistance, the listener's desire is also on trial.

Is the conflict one of risking learning before one knows what will happen to desire? What disasters are being anticipated and what wishes are being destroyed? Are words themselves the problem? We can notice that each fragment of life in education is drenched in a sea of anxiety. There are institutional imperatives and resistance to meeting them. And the stories are not quite stories. Like the dream, their pieces are incomplete and mismatched. We do not yet know where danger lurks: in the story of defeat or with our responses to them? And there are so many ways to fail. Beneath their surface awaits familiar disappointment with the self, followed by the need to be punished: kidney stones, being caught in a lie, plagiarism, and bad grades.

Such ordinary narratives give a partial account of the suspended self. And it seems as if only literature has the patience to dwell in its sadness. T. S. Eliot's (1917) poem "The Love-Song of J. Alfred Prufrock" gives words to this holding back with the terrible question, "Do I dare disturb the universe?" Herman Melville's short story "Bartleby, the Scrivener: A Story of Wall Street" already has an answer in Bartleby's negation: "I would prefer not to." This sentence, for the story's narrator, holds quiet mysteries. It draws him to Bartleby. And the narrator who writes this vague report admits: "For the first time in my life a feeling of overpowering stinging melancholy seized me" (Melville 1997, 33). The narrator feels what Bartleby feels: lost, helpless, and bereft.

With resistance, desire is held in suspense. The self is caught between wishes for goodness and the terror of mistakes. Things do not add up; even as thought-events escalate, they only leave in their wake defeated equations. They can barely be explained by ordinary logic and their effects elude their cause. They may even be an attack on meaning. Left alone, these part narratives emote painful absence. Like the dream, they are in the service of congealed communication and disguised wishes. For, after all, constructing significance risks the self's ideality and gambles with uncertainty. Constructing significance may take us to the limits of education.

Given its sliding nature, the handling of resistance proposes problems of interpretation. I'll point to three. First, resistance is contagious, and this transference affects its interpretation. Addressing resistance often gets caught in the immediacy of the felt encounter, and typically, resistance is met with authoritarian actions on both sides. Learning is thus equated with having to be punished. A second slide is with the nature of resistance, what Freud pointed out in his ironic concept, 'resistance to resistance.' We don't want resistance to be admitted as our reason for not being able to change. But also telling someone that she is only resisting is of no help. So the interpretation cannot take the side of certitude or authoritarian explanations. Resistance to resistance is usually carried on through the ego defenses of intellectualization, rationalization, denial, undoing what has already happened, and projective identifications. Perhaps what is most ordinary about this resistance is the instance that emotional life is meaningless. And the third slide is that interpreting resistance brings us into the difficulties of communication since resistance destroys responsibility and agonizes narcissistic wounds. For all these reasons, the approach to resistance must take the path of least resistance.

A closer listening for quiet, ordinary, and painful resistance, the sort that may first annoy educators, may remind us of our own helplessness, and, then bring us to choose the uncertain path of symbolization. Ethically, we can ask, What can the educator learn from resistance to learning? And this means trying to describe an unconscious geometry of the educator's transference that also leans on identifications and other ego defense mechanisms. Perhaps the most difficult question for teachers, whether they work in schools or universities, is this: What would be a non-defensive way to understand and work through our own resistance to learning?

Winnicott's Consultations: The Adolescent And The Teacher

For D.W. Winnicott (1991), the psychotherapist acts as if he or she is a mirror for the patient's expressions. We know that a mirror does not resist the image but is only a reflection of a surface. One can even say, to return to Kierkegaard, that the mirror is another qualification of subjectivity. Yet Winnicott advises that to mirror the other also means trying to understand what the other has difficulty meeting. This brings us to the question of resistance and desire. I'll illustrate Winnicott's path of least resistance in two of his clinical cases, one having to do with an adolescent girl called Sarah and the other with a teacher who remains nameless. They both concern difficulties with being in school.

Sarah was sixteen years old when her parents brought her to Winnicott for a consultation. He had seen her fourteen years before, and Sarah had a vague memory of that play session, recalling that as a young child, she yelled and yelled.

Sarah readily admits to Winnicott that she does not understand her feelings and has difficulty controlling her outbursts. She attributes her difficulties to just growing up and believes that once she can get through the thickets of adolescence, she will be all right. Her mother told her she would feel better once she had her own philosophy. Sarah tells Winnicott in the middle of the session that she sometimes lies and does not work hard in school. She says, "I'm all the time trying to make an impression because I'm not sure enough of myself. I've been like it for ages. I can't remember being anything else" (Winnicott 1991,122). Winnicott writes: "I said: It's sad, isn't it?—as a way of showing that I had heard what she said and that I had feelings because of the implications of what she was telling me" (122). This is what Winnicott means by communication: that Sarah does not have to perform because her feelings are impressions and they do affect the other.

Sarah described entering a new school: "I felt worthless, and also I was scared physically. I expected to be stabbed, shot, or strangled. Especially stabbed. Like having something pinned on your back, and you didn't know" (Winnicott 1991, 125). She felt she could not depend on anyone and her friends kept changing and turning against her. It is at this point that Winnicott offers an interpretation of the session:

> The depression means something, something unconscious. [I could use this word with this girl.] You hate the dependable person who has changed and who has ceased to be understanding and dependable, and has perhaps become vindictive. You became depressed instead of feeling hate of the person who was reliable but who changed. (1991, 125)

Sarah then tells Winnicott she was sent home from boarding school and this is the reason she is seeing him. She is about to meet her own unreliability.

The incident Sarah describes is quite fantastical. Her story has the quality of a dream. She did not yet know that she was telling her story all along, but the incident picks up the threads of hostility she felt from others and reverses her worries that she would be 'stabbed in the back.'

There was a woman, one of the school's housemothers, whom Sarah hated. This housemother reminded Sarah of what she hated in herself. The woman is self-centered, vain, unreliable, and does not do work. This woman seems to stay behind a door and would not open it. So Sarah took a knife and threw it against the door. And the woman walks into the room and asks Sarah if she has lost her mind. Sarah made up a lie and told the woman she was only fixing the door. Things escalated further as the woman demanded that Sarah take off her hat. Sarah says, "Why should I?" and the woman says, "Because I told you to." Then Sarah screams and screams and screams, and the woman says, "OK, scream more!" (1991, 126) And Sarah did. It is at this point that Winnicott recalls Sarah's first visit to him fourteen years ago. She screamed and screamed.

The question is how to make sense of this jumbled material. Resistance, after all, does not come with directions as to how it can be handled. Winnicott's approach is to stay with Sarah's feelings of betrayal: that good people can turn into bad ones. He places Sarah's convictions on this matter into her childhood during her mother's pregnancy, when Sarah was no longer able to sit on her mother's lap. Sarah felt her mother had changed from being reliable to unreliable. Sarah carried her disillusionment into the school events: the housemother was not reliable. And in the knife-throwing incident, Sarah had managed to make the housemother into a bad mother.

There is quite a bit going on here, and we should not leap into solutions or judgments. We can notice where Sarah's logic crumbles; there are unconscious meanings to Sarah's outburst, and these can be sorted out and made into significance. We can also notice that Sarah felt locked out and wanted to change the lock. But these are not yet desires, and it is here that Winnicott risks significance.

Winnicott (1991) tells Sarah:

> 'OK, but I do want you to know that I can see one thing you can't see and that is that your anger is with a good and not a bad woman. The good woman changes to bad.' Sarah replied, 'That is mother isn't it, but mother is absolutely all right now.' Winnicott then replies: 'Yes, it's in the pattern in the dream that you can't remember that you destroy your good dependable mother. Your job will be to live through some relationships that do go a bit bad, when you do become a bit angry and a bit disillusioned, and somehow everyone survives.' (128)

Typically, Winnicott does not give long interpretations. But his language was simple to the effect that he wished Sarah to consider how she worries that good experience will turn bad and that she will try to make this happen before it happens to her. He was working from the idea of psychoanalysis on demand and did not know if he would see Sarah again. In a way, he is also disillusioning one of his own beliefs: that the patient must come to her own meaning and has the right to take her own time. So there is a great deal of meaning, perhaps with the hope that some of it could be received, such as the job we each have, namely, to live through relationships that go a bit bad. I think he was also addressing the adolescent's dilemma, containing the good and the bad in such a way that everyone survives. One of the surprising turns in this case is that Winnicott agrees that Sarah can take time away from school. Sometimes limiting education is the path of least resistance.

Winnicott's second case concerns a female teacher, age forty. He does not relate the teacher to Sarah but there is an irony of a student and a teacher sharing the same dilemma of something being unreliable and worries that good things turn bad.

The teacher described her sorrow as being unable "to stand in the other person's shoes" (Winnicott 1991, 131). She had difficulty feeling what another person was feeling and believed that others could not know how she felt. Essentially, feelings were meaningless. I think we are approaching questions of resistance to feelings, a private affair that brings a great many disappointments. The irony is that the teacher could identify with distant others whom she could not actually contact or help. She cared a great deal for the oppressed people of the world, including women who she saw as always being degraded. The problem is not that this teacher is right about the world's treatment of women. The issue is what happens to this knowledge and how it leaves the teacher bereft. In a nutshell, the teacher becomes the bad, wrecked woman whom everyone ignores.

A second irony is that this teacher has many opportunities to see the bad parts of herself in her students. And one might speculate that putting oneself into the other's shoes feels like compliance. The teacher is no stranger to education: in fact, like every teacher, she spent her childhood and adolescence there. In a sense, we could say that her identifications languished in the waiting room of education. The work, as Winnicott sees it, is to expand identifications to imagine what other people are like in order to understand what it is like to be a self.

Gradually, this teacher began to speak of her disparity to wonder what is in front of her eyes. Winnicott (1991) wrote, "My patient was able to see with scarcely any help at all from the analyst that these children were not living for her benefit, although she had felt that they were doing exactly that" (134). Resistance feels like a fight between affect and idea, where one both knows and does not know and where one wishes to disturb the universe but prefers not to. The analytic work, however, urges movement, permitting the patient to step into the analyst's shoes and essentially learn how to merge, walk away, and survive. The teacher's imagination is her mirror for understanding others, even if it sometimes refracts old preconceptions, handmade from childhood and adolescent affairs.

The Irony of Working Through

To imagine the mind of the other risks one's own mind. Freud's advice is to try to be completely honest with oneself. The irony is that this work is qualified by intersubjectivity and then the door opens onto uncertainty. We can say that resistance closes the door of possible meanings. Freud (1913) furthers this irony when he places resistance into the heart of the psychical world. He had more advice for educators in a 1913 paper in which he speculated on resistance within the pedagogical relation:

> Only someone who can feel his way into the minds of children can be capable of educating them; and we grown-up people cannot understand children because we no longer understand our own childhood. Our infantile amnesia proves that we have grown estranged from our childhood. (189)

One's own childhood education is difficult to remember for so many reasons, and to return the irony of Freud's observation, there must be an estrangement between teachers and students since they are different people and difference is another qualification of intersubjectivity. Understanding this estrangement, Freud felt, could lead educators into an analysis of their own repressions, another term for resistance to learning. At the time of these remarks on the educator's estrangement from the student, Freud argued that significant forgetting had to do with the repression of sexuality. It is not so much that we forget the childhood sexual researches as much as we ignore what it feels like to want thrilling, impossible knowledge and persist in making unassailable theories. This forgetting is also the teacher's resistance to her or his own desires. Perhaps the greatest desire at stake is the desire for pedagogical imagination that includes the capacity to tolerate incompatible ideas resistance holds in store. This is the great irony of working through psychical inertia: not only must we remember what we forget, but the recollection must also take us beyond the neurosis of repeating our memories of education.

If we return to the four dreamy fragments of ordinary, painful, and quiet resistance for a moment, we can see that that resistance has as much to do with the self as it does with the other, even as it is felt as desire's inhibition and, in some sense, as a fear of freedom. In each case, all that might be good turns bad. My sense is that individuals worried about how they may be received and mirrored. The ironic movement would be to step into their shoes without stepping on their toes.

The psychical events of resistance as a difficult communication and as requiring symbolization, or mirroring, may open our imagination into what it is like to be frightened of learning, authorship, intersubjectivity, and desire and why we need to reflect, in our responses, the interest in learning, authorship, intersubjectivity, and desire. Here we gamble with meaning. In the overabundant studio of resistance, we would do best to take the path of least resistance.

Bibliography

Eliot, Thomas Sterns. 1917. *Prufrock and Other Observations*. London: The Egoist.

Freud, Anna. (1930) 1974. "Four Lectures on Psychoanalysis for Teachers and Parents." In *The Writings of Anna Freud, Vol. 1, 1922–1935*, 73–133. New York: International Universities Press.

Freud, Sigmund. 1953–1974. *The Standard Edition of the Complete Psychological Works of Sigmund Freud*, edited and translated by James Strachey, in collaboration with Anna Freud. 24 vols. London: Hogarth Press and Institute for Psychoanalysis.

———. 1897. "Letter 71 (October 15, 1897)." In *The Standard Edition of the Complete Psychological Works of Sigmund Freud*, edited and translated by James Strachey, in collaboration with Anna Freud, vol. 1, 263–66. London: Hogarth Press and Institute for Psychoanalysis.

———. 1913. "The Claims of Psycho-Analysis to Scientific Interest." In *The Standard Edition of the Complete Psychological Works of Sigmund Freud*, edited and translated by James Strachey, in collaboration with Anna Freud, vol. 13, 163–90. London: Hogarth Press and Institute for Psychoanalysis.

———. 1914. "Remembering, Repeating and Working-Through (Further Recommendations on the Technique of Psycho-Analysis II)." In *The Standard Edition of the Complete Psychological Works of Sigmund Freud*, edited and translated by James Strachey, in collaboration with Anna Freud, vol. 12, 145–56. London: Hogarth Press and Institute for Psychoanalysis.

Kierkegaard, Søren. (1861) 1989. *The Concept of Irony with Continual Reference to Socrates*. Edited and translated by Howard V. Hong and Edna H. Hong. Princeton, NJ: Princeton University Press.

Kristeva, Julia. 2009. *This Incredible Need to Believe*. Translated by Beverley Bie Brahic. New York: Columbia University Press.

Lear, Jonathan. 2003. *Therapeutic Action: An Earnest Plea for Irony*. New York: The Other Press.

Melville, Herman. 1997. "Bartleby, the Scrivener: A Story of Wall Street." In *The Complete Shorter Fiction by Herman Melville*, 18–51. New York: Alfred A. Knopf.

Winnicott, Donald. W. 1991. "Interrelating Apart from Instinctual Drive and in Terms of Cross-Identifications." In *Playing and Reality*, 119–137. New York: Routledge Press.

CHAPTER 12

'Even in Cambridge'

IT IS HARD to imagine what it was like at the start of the twentieth century to first encounter the Freudian subject of sexuality, the unconscious, dreams, and infantile life. Just as difficult to grasp was the psychoanalytic situation of the unconscious: that the flux and flummox of psychical life can be interpreted, as Freud ([1900] 1968) announced with his *Interpretation of Dreams*. And who would have known how to present the risk of imagination made from dream life? Who then would have dared to consider dreams as altering the course of the interpretation of education? And what new methods of research open the study of the history of Freud's reception?

Freud in Cambridge is John Forrester and Laura Cameron's (2017) remarkable history of a cohorts' early enthusiasm for the novelties of psychoanalysis, assessed through the lives of mostly men who endlessly documented their intricate relations, fights, competitions, and love affairs. Within these men's youthful enthusiasm for Freud, readers learn of their attempts to understand more deeply the urgency, irruptions, anguish, false leads, and twists and turns of their own mental states and relations to others. They hoped for a new kind of self, perhaps as a wish for transcendence brought on by "first love." Their lost hope was for a new kind of education, one capable of being affected by the passions of human activity. What these men could not account for was why and how passion may overturn the ways science, objectivity, measurement, and, of course, education can be imagined.

The heart of Forrester and Cameron's (2017) study concerns the subjective factor that belongs to any human creation: "This analogy will remind us that in writing the history of psychoanalysis, passions, secret loves and deep inner troubles will play, even in Cambridge, as important a part as the architecture of scientific theory, the foundations of a scientific discipline or the proper way to educate the next generation" (6). My remarks focus this last element: the history of writing into deeply felt conflicts over "the proper way to educate the next generation."

Questions on the meaning of life felt through emotional dismay over inchoateness of dreams, discontentment, jealously, aimlessness, inhibitions, and depression brought many Cambridge figures to travel to Vienna to be analyzed by Freud or to Berlin with Karl Abraham. The migration to psychoanalysis occurred between 1922 and 1928 and then, psychoanalysis seemed to have disappeared from a Cambridge overtaken by social conservatism, the rise of experimental psychology, and perhaps, the University's turn to natural science and away from the rise of literary modernism and its demand to disrupt experience (510). After 1930, psychoanalytic study moved mainly into psychoanalytic institutes for clinical training. But in the beginning, it would only take a dream for some to drop everything and go to psychoanalysis.

And it happened that a group of people, living within or at a distance of "the most science-oriented university," (4) found their surprising interests by opening the vault of knowledge orthodoxies to their dreams of education and hence opening the disciplines of science to the otherness of psychoanalytic situations found in subjectivity, freedom, sexuality, and the unconscious. The dilemma is that these psychical factors, then and now, are incompatible with and even obstacles to the push for authority, expertise, power, and professionalization that also qualify the changing university. Where psychoanalysis was able to take root was in the methods on offer, and so the main effects were still in education, but tucked into the substratum which left the idea of education behind, namely within the history of the rise of the disciplines of anthropology, literary theory, economics, sociology, criminology, and philosophy. If we looked carefully at the foundational methodologies of these human disciplines from participant observation in anthropology to ethnographic verstehen, from close readings, practical criticism, and a psychology of reading to the interest in misunderstandings as found in literary studies, and, if we looked to the migration of psychoanalytic vocabulary to all these disciplinary endeavors, from all of this we would find traces of psychoanalysis. However, Forrester and Cameron (2017) are quite clear on the outcome of their study: "What did not happen was that psychoanalysis became a University discipline ... [and] wild enthusiasm turned into calculated quarantining, both within the University and without" (630).

The issue for education is that groups of people have to be affected by new ideas and carry these ideas further. But the ideas themselves do not determine where they land. Forrester and Cameron (2017) approach education by what they see as a laboratory for the study of human conduct and this is one of the best definitions of education that may open its repressions. These authors are interested in the fate of ideas. Their method for tracing the migration and dissemination of ideas is prosopographical: "a collective study of the lives of a group, a population, a cohort ... links between multiple 'life-lines'" (5). And so, where the contingencies of human situations play an inordinate role in the creation of theory and the drama of their lives ... there, history will become. Loves, losses, jealousies, defenses, and wishes, for example, leave a residue of phantasy that animates the designs and reception of theory and practice. Psychoanalysts know this transference situation well, and yet even well-known knowledge has a tendency to disappear, to go without saying, to be integrated into invisibility, and to be misunderstood. After all, what begins as a dream will be difficult to remember.

The questions that structure Forrester and Cameron's (2017) study continue as predicaments for the human problem of studies in education: What happens when we try to change something stultifying in our lives, and even, because of our encounter with psychoanalytic movement, what happens when we imagine doing what could not have been done before? What is compelling or moving about the psychoanalytic adventure? Why turn to and then away from psychoanalysis and use both directions of here/gone to say something about ourselves, our education, and our world? And can psychoanalysis be the basis for imagining an education of human conduct, including the destructive and sexual drives?

Perhaps the irony is that those who went into analysis with Freud or were influenced by Freudian practices may have had their individual epiphanies. While many brought psychoanalytic orientations to their academic disciplines, they also moved on. And Freud never came to Cambridge. Cambridge, it turned out, would not and could not become the great educational experiment. Then and now, psychoanalysis barely has a toehold in university life.

And yet there was indeed a great educational experiment in Cambridge in the backyard so to say. It had to do with a dream for "the proper education for the next generation," founded by a father parent, Geoffrey Pyke, who started the short-lived Malting House Garden School for the children of Cambridge professors. I imagine it as a kind of anti-Cambridge, one of the precursors to linking education with what is most radical about passionate subjectivity. The Malting House Garden School was one of the first experiments to take inspiration from Freudian views on group life, upbringing, imagination, sexuality, and sublimation of drives. At least between 1924 and 1927, children of professors had free reign to project their love and hate into unconventional teaching and learning. And their teachers, particularly Susan Issacs would go on to be known as that great defender of Kleinian phantasy during the 1940–42 Controversial Discussions of the British Psychoanalytical Society in London. Many of the teachers in the Malting School were active in the Society. Melanie Klein came to the Malting Garden when she briefly visited Cambridge and may have held a consult with Pyke's son. James Strachey also visited the school. He expressed dismay at the children's messy bodies and aggressive tendencies given free play. The university, however, took no interest in the school.

The Malting House Garden School was the laboratory of human conduct made by free-thinking parents influenced by life science in Cambridge and the sexual experiments in Bloomsbury. This combine is quite significant as Bloomsbury in London was a community of modernism, with literary, sexual, and artistic experimentations. Hogarth Press, owned by Leonard and Virginia Woolf, published translations from German to English of Freud's work, and Cameron and Forrester argued that the Freudian influence on education "helped to foster both an atmosphere of psychoanalytic experimentation and a reforming zeal linked to women's rights, sex, and access to birth control" (Forrester and Cameron 2017, 436). One can see psychoanalysis siding with social reform with the idea that material conditions founded in educational campaigns are needed for the capacity to narrate, think, and revolt.

As for the school, there was a deep adult wish for children to have a childhood free of neurosis; indeed, while no adult actually had this experience, the wish to create a happy education, devoid of authoritarianism and without isolating the child from the larger world, was a radically new idea. It was also a wish to link science to the imagination, something Freud ([1900] 1968) did in his book on dream interpretation and what he continued to do in every public lecture he gave when he explained resistance to psychoanalysis (Britzman 2011). As for the school, radically new education was a strange and perhaps estranging combination: there was the child's discovery as experienced in the physical sciences, engineering, and the natural world; there was the child's exploration and enactments of emotions, particularly aggressive and melancholy states of mind; and, for the adults, there was a near anthropological enthusiasm for observing and documenting children's actions as if they were a tiny culture just discovered. Observations were also grist for the psychoanalytic mill. As for the teachers, their school philosophy attempted to diminish the pedagogical tendency toward the exercise of arbitrary power, punitive discipline, and compliance, all features of Cambridge University. A new problem could then be imagined. Does the ideal of turning children into "little scientists" also mean that there would be an overcoming of emotional life? And, if the parents could not overcome their own neurosis, would it even be possible for their children to escape? We do know then as in now, that education must be a rough-and-tumble play, that it cannot proceed without psychical conflict, but these are also the situations that can stop education short, particularly if, in social life, the unconscious forces of the subjective factors of love and hate are denied. And, as for the school, the adult trade of love and hate ultimately left in its wake bad feelings, petty jealously, and no insight into the nature of human nature, even in Cambridge.

The Malting House Garden School only lasted three years. So, the rise and fall of education is also a part of the trace Freud left with Cambridge. Much of what can be known of this school, thought about as an education against inhibition, is due to Susan Issacs's three books on child development that drew upon her work there between 1924 and 1927. Issacs, by the way, did spend some time in Cambridge as a researcher assistant in 1912–13. She felt women were treated as intruders (Forrester and Cameron 2017, 444). And so, too, were children. In a sense, Issacs's books may have suffered the same fate as did Freud in the field of education; Forrester and Cameron (2017) note that these books "containing cross-indexed detailed evidence supporting infantile sexuality in its oral, anal, and genital phases, particularly unsettled the nursey education world" (435). We can observe the same fear of emotional life in contemporary resistances to both psychoanalysis and to the messy bodies in education.

What remains are the ways we think about psychoanalysis and education. In my little book *Freud and Education* (Britzman 2011), I tried to show not only Freud's thinking about education but how the concept of education is subtly woven against the grain of Freudian theory. Freud's approach was to stay with the difficulties in and resistances to teaching and learning. His was an education by obstacle. Freud, we know, thought the education of children should be separate from psychoanalysis and he did call psychoanalysis for adults "after education." Anna Freud stayed rather close to education in her thinking that the role of the child analyst, as with the teacher, is to be a universal superego and help the child move closer to reality. Melanie Klein thought otherwise. Klein gave up on the idea that there should be a pedagogical value to child analysis. She argued that the only goal should be an interest in the meaning of phantasy and the freeing of the inner world from ancient grievances and hostilities (Klein 1921). The Malting School tried to contain these divergent themes, and it still is the case that ongoing debates cannot settle the issue of whether psychoanalysis and education are compatible. Nor can these debates settle the problem of what reality can be for education. Perhaps the best we can do is explore these as elemental dilemmas given that the human, in order to think at all, may need conflicts between reality and phantasy, self and other, and perception and object.

I read Forrester and Cameron's (2017) conclusion to their study as ending on a sad note and there are two parts to my sadness. One has to do with the repression of Freudian theory in the creation of the fields of anthropology, sociology, economics, literary studies, philosophy, and education. I often wonder what would it mean for the university to give Freud his due? And what new debates might then be made? A second sadness involves some speculation on what Cambridge gave up on in order to preserve its grip on the meaning of science. Forrester and Cameron described an ongoing problem of education and perhaps of psychoanalysis too, namely, "how wild enthusiasm became a case of calculated quarantining, both within the university and without" (630). We don't really know what sustains interest though we are more adept at cutting interest short. If there is a lesson here, it may begin by us noticing that Forrester and Cameron's book was, after all, published by Cambridge University Press, and by a stroke of fate or really by their dedicated and brilliant study, these authors did indeed give Cambridge back into the hands of Sigmund Freud.

Bibliography

Britzman, Deborah P. 2011. *Freud and Education*. New York: Routledge Press.
Forrester, John and Laura Cameron. 2017. *Freud in Cambridge*. Cambridge: Cambridge University Press.
Freud, Sigmund. (1900) 1968. "The Interpretation of Dreams (First Part)." In *The Standard Edition of the Complete Psychological Works of Sigmund Freud, Volume IV (1900): The Interpretation of Dreams (First Part)*, edited and translated by James Strachey, in collaboration with Anna Freud, 1–338. London: Hogarth Press.
Klein, Melanie. (1921) 1975. "The Development of a Child." In *Love, Guilt and Reparation and Other Works 1921-1945*. Pp. 1–53. London: Hogarth Press.

CHAPTER 13

What Is Emotional About Our Emotional Situation?

You will not find the term *emotional situation* in any of the psychoanalytic dictionaries. It is not a technique but rather serves as a touching index, such as *see under:* baby, breast, good versus bad, constellations of anxiety, formation of the dynamic state of the inner world, functions of protean urgencies, object relations, affects in, phantasies of, play, inner and outer relationships to, symptoms of, and the desire to know. The full phrase that belongs to Melanie Klein's ([1959] 1975) formulation reads as "the emotional situation of the baby." And it is the situation of dependency, vulnerability, and interest that allows emotions to be understood as if in relation to someone or some object. In her study of Klein, Julia Kristeva (2001) described the child's emotional situation through Klein's understanding of play: "Play . . . is not the abstract dramatization of "objects" of desire or of hatred symbolized by toys. Klein's conception of play is rooted in the body and the world: play exists to the extent that it moves forward, burns, breaks, wipes, dirties, cleans, destroys, constructs, and so forth" (49). My understanding is that Kristeva's frame of Kleinian play may be compared to what happens in writing from any confrontation with the objects of learning. Here, I extend these Kleinian dynamics into 'the emotional situation of education' and consider their lines of flight to create new thoughts on life and case study writing.

Klein ([1959] 1975) dates the human's emotional situation from the beginning of life and finds its infantile roots in the world of the adult. Her formulation is that the course of emotional life for both the child and later for the adult "is influenced by earliest emotions and unconscious phantasies . . . and, that the newborn baby experiences, both in the process of birth and in the adjustment to postnatal situation, anxiety of a persecutory nature. . . . This can be explained by the fact that the young infant, without being able to grasp it intellectually, feels unconsciously every discomfort as though it were inflicted on him by hostile forces" (248). The key situations are bodily ones: discomfort, inchoateness, pain, frustration, burning, rage, and feeling something good has suddenly turned bad. These hated experiences take the form of persecutory anxiety, hostile phantasies, and numerous defenses against them. Such dynamics may also be relevant to our theories of learning since it is the case that whenever we met new experiences and ideas that cannot rely on or affirm what we already know, whenever we feel the difficulties of changing one's mind as the breaking heart of changing the self, our first line of defense is to deny the possibility of meaning, relevance, or interest. It all feels like the 'adjustment to postnatal situation.'

Admittedly, Klein is hard to take in and not only due to her insistence on unconscious life and that the adult mind has its roots in infancy. Her writing on phantasies, anxieties, and defenses serves as the raw nerves of affect, and reading Klein can feel as one's mind teeters on the brink between the denial of pain and the poignancy of thinking. The difficulty concerns how we grasp the destiny of anxiety; for Klein, its mechanism is the transference of emotional situations, first into objects, good and bad, and then as dispersal into objects of interest. Klein understands the designs of object relations as not only the foundation for imagination, personalization, identification, and symbolization but also our relations to others near and far as projective identifications. The designs of object relations serve as our soft spot.

My summary leads me to ask two psychoanalytic questions: What is the backdrop of conflicts that push one to write case studies from the emotional situation of education? And, how may we represent emotional situations through the transference?

John Forrester's (2016) *Thinking with Cases* provides an opening gambit: reading and writing lean on our emotional situation with having to symbolize the qualities and logic of anxieties. Forrester points to a Freudian crisis for the writer and reader: "Psychoanalytic writing is not just writing *about* psychoanalysis; it is a writing subject to the same laws and processes as the psychoanalytic situation itself. In this way psychoanalysis can never free itself of the forces it attempts to describe" (65). Furthermore, psychoanalytic writing opens a startling paradox caught in psychoanalytic functions: while transference has as its passion an attachment to both an object thought and person, due to its symptomatic nature, it is also affected by a failure to transmit. As affectivity, transference is also an enactment of miscommunication, founded on desire. Forrester proposes an impossible quest: "Ordinary readers of texts and ordinary folk engaged in social intercourse may on occasion bemoan the fact that there is no interpretation-free zone of human relations; similarly, psychoanalysts and their critics may bemoan the fact that there is no transference-free zone of description of these relations" (66). Putting these complaints into one syndrome, one can note that transference, or the ways we give ourselves over to extending our emotional situation into the lives of others and the way we bring objects closer to us or send them running away, is already a nascent interpretation, albeit an unconscious one. There is no knowledge of human development that can exceed our mental acts and emotional life gives us our relations to reason, belief, confidence, conflict, ambivalence, confusion, and anguish. And, there is no transference free zone for readers or writers.

We might then understand psychical life as symptomatic in that it works to effectuate or perhaps even constitute the subjective contingencies of the human necessity for education that always involve dependency, vulnerability, separation, and difference. Emotional situations, as delegates of affect, are both claimed and disclaimed. I think about the disclaimed aspect of the emotional world through a particular problem we face in any education that can be described as the defense of mental concreteness and the disavowal of the self's contribution to foreclosing the other's difference and one's self-difference (Bass 2000). Another way of putting this limit is through Melanie Klein's ([1946] 1975) view that the most devastating manic defense, perhaps because it is the earliest, is the denial of the reach, force, and significance of psychical reality as the life of the mind. Denial that psychical life matters is, I think, a way to destroy the mind on the way to destroying the minds of others. What then does transference have to do with the make up our emotional situation?

Looking closer at this emotional situation, Hanna Segal developed the idea that pathos and creativity go hand in hand. Segal's ([1952] 2004) early paper on psychoanalysis and aesthetics, written just after the Second World War, dramatized the writer's passage: "It is when the world within us is destroyed, when it is dead and loveless, when our loved ones are in fragments, and we ourselves in helpless despair—it is then that we must re-create our world anew, reassemble the pieces, infuse life into dead fragments, re-create life" (47). Segal turns to the inside of mental space and imagination, envisioning the self, as that struggle to sustain affecting words for all that is lost.

Putting oneself together again, however, leads to numerous anxieties. Melanie Klein's ([1935] 1975) provides an emotional description of the chaotic scenes of trying to recreate our inner world:

> To quote only a few of them: there is anxiety how to put the bits together in the right way and at the right time; how to pick out the good bits and do away with the bad ones; how to bring the object to life when it has been put together; and there is the anxiety of being interfered with in this task by bad objects and by one's own hatred, etc. (269)

For Klein, reparation also proposes the fear of continuing to damage. What if the pieces of life cannot hold the story? And I think this transference anxiety, both negative and positive, may be not only the biographer's flight from identification but also the means into her study. We do have to feel our way into ideas but in doing that, we may mistake our feelings for the idea we encounter.

Elisabeth Young-Bruehl's (1998) *Subject to Biography: Psychoanalysis, Feminism, and Writing Women's Lives* remains an exemplar for the question of "identificatory engagement" (24), or 'modest' empathy that permits inquiry into the nature of this mental projective identification and its transference into the object of study. Young-Bruehl was the accidental biographer of Hannah Arendt and then the chosen one for Anna Freud. Between these figures, Young-Bruehl opens her way into the thorny question of the biographer's relation to the life of the other and the intermixing of identification and difference. How does the biographer's transference play out in the writing? Young-Bruehl strongly attached to Hannah Arendt, mind to mind. Arendt was, after all, her teacher and dissertation supervisor. And after the death of Arendt, Arendt's family approached Young-Bruehl with the request to write the biography. While Young-Bruehl had some assumptions as to the roots of Arendt's passion for the mind, she admitted the need for displacement: "worked out in the medium of history and a historical-biographical narrative. Arendt played in my mind the role of the legitimator of a quest for understanding" (23). We can say that the transference was positive, "mind to mind." Young-Bruehl did not feel that way toward Anna Freud, particularly on the matter of what she thought of Anna Freud's desire: "I said, this is not the desire that determines my relationships with women or with men, this is a desire that I find frightening even to think about—*so it must be mine in a way that I do not yet understand.* Her need sent me on a self-quest" (23).

Somewhere between the quest for understanding, notably outward-looking, and the quest for self, notably inward-looking, one may find the situation of not understanding, and from there, the idea that to understand at all brings a change for the self. Furthermore, the obstacle to claiming one's own emotional situation becomes a methodology of biography. Young-Bruehl (1998) formulated her case study method as a relation: "empathy to difference. Not simple empathy, but overcoming-antipathy, a kind of second-order or reinforced empathy for what is forever foreign in another" (21). And what is "forever foreign" is the unconscious. Young-Bruehl had to admit disagreement with Anna Freud's incontrovertible homophobia. How does one write the story that breaks the heart of the biographer? Difficult questions follow: Should our strong critique, our disagreements, and our splitting, lead us away from the lives of others? Or is there a self-division, an otherness within, in any learning that may be apprehended and used? As Young-Bruehl immersed herself in Anna Freud's world, something softened. It had to do with respecting a gap between the self and the other, and from this gap, Young-Bruehl develops empathy and tenderness, an emotional tie she terms "identificatory engagement" that does include the pain of recognition. Young-Bruehl's emotional tie is quite close to Klein's discussion of a new anxiety in postnatal life: the depressive position. There, one can come to terms with the pain of incompleteness that also accompanies any effort at understanding self with other.

I experienced the transference conflicts Young-Bruehl described as I wrote my case studies of Freud and Klein (Britzman 2011, 2016). Freud did serve as my intellectual legitimator in the sense of permitting my interest in play, speculation, interpretation, history, and new questions. I felt something different with Klein. Her psychoanalysis that emphasized the earliest years as our emotional situation, scared me. Only later could I see her as my emotional legitimator, and only then could I accept my sway between incoherence and the pain of incompleteness. These are also the sways between my paranoid-schizoid and depressive positions. It was really from Klein that I came to understand why psychoanalysis is talking about us, why we are charged with trying to address something within us all that we know nothing about, and why emotions are a situation. My persecutory anxiety could soften when I acknowledged that what scares me is mine.

Klein left us with the questions of love and hate, envy and gratitude, and guilt and reparation. She gives to us the idea that depression, anxiety, and phantasies are the volatile tenders of any education as much as they are the compost of the earliest years of our emotional situations in dependency, helplessness, and love (Klein 1946/1975). And this emotional situation with all others renders our boundaries with others fragile, subject to the defense of concreteness, confusion, and symbolic collapse. Empathy to difference and empathy with tenderness are late developments; these arrive only when, as Young-Bruehl pointed out, frightening ideas can be mine. To return to Forrester's counsel, everything depends on the apprehension that there is no transference-free zone. And just as there is no unaffected body-free zone, whether claimed or disclaimed, for education, there is no emotional situation-free zone.

Bibliography

Bass, Alan. 2000. *Difference and Disavowal: The Trauma of Eros.* Stanford, CA: Stanford University Press.

Britzman, Deborah P. 2011. *Freud and Education.* New York: Routledge Press.

———.2016. *Melanie Klein: Early Analysis, Play and the Question of Freedom.* New York: Springer Press.

Forrester, John. 2016. *Thinking in Cases.* Cambridge, UK: Polity Books.

Klein, Melanie. (1935) 1975. "A Contribution to the Psychogenesis of Manic-Depressive States." In *Love, Guilt and Reparation and Other Works, 1921–1945,* 290–305. London: Hogarth Press.

———. (1946) 1975. "Notes on Some Schizoid Mechanisms." In *Envy and Gratitude and Other Works, 1946–1963,* 1–24. London: Hogarth Press.

———. (1959) 1975. "Our Adult World and Its Roots in Infancy." In *Envy and Gratitude and Other Works, 1946–1963,* 247–65. London: Hogarth Press.

Kristeva, Julia. 2001. *Melanie Klein.* Translated by Ross Guberman. New York: Columbia University Press.

Segal, Hanna. (1952) 2004. "A Psychoanalytic Approach to Aesthetics." In *Psychoanalysis and Art: Kleinian Perspectives,* edited by Sandra Gosso, 42–61. London: Karnac Books.

Young-Bruehl, Elizabeth. 1998. *Subject to Biography: Psychoanalysis, Feminism, and Writing Women's Lives.* Cambridge, MA: Harvard University Press.

CHAPTER 14

On Disquieting Imagination, Indeterminacy, Aesthetic Conflicts, And Grouch Days

MORE THAN THIRTY years ago, Maxine Greene (1986) returned us to an elemental dilemma in her essay "In Search of Critical Pedagogy." Her discussion occurred at a time when many of us thought that finally, critical pedagogy had arrived! But we were only at the beginning and had not yet felt the internal sting of self-criticism. Greene had the courage to ask: "What are the sources of questioning, of restlessness? How are we to move the young to break with the given and taken-for-granted—to move toward what might be, what is not yet?" (427). And, mostly, her answer was that to think we have to search for what is not yet. It may be missing, it may be absence, it may be lack, it may be denial, it may be a lost object, and it may also be possibilities, a perhaps, and an openness to what is not known. It may involve the unknown and the unknowable. I add to this search an analytic position of 'negative capability' that can accompany disquieting imagination. The poet John Keats used that phrase in a letter to his brother and described the labor of imagination: "that is when man is capable of being in uncertainties, Mysteries, doubts, without any irritable reaching after fact and reason" (Forman 1960, 71).

Without irritation, thinking is that experiment with thoughts of uncertainty, and there, for those interested in learning psychoanalytic views, facts and reasons may not be as convincing as the questions we are able to ask. In a graduate seminar in psychoanalytic theory, I was asked about Melanie Klein's view of the emotional world. Why, a student demanded, would anxiety serve as the basis for symbolization? What does anxiety have to do with love and hate? And what does anxiety have to do with the loss of the breast? Now these are searching questions but also anxious ones. Such questions take me to take the side of the netherworld of phantasy that, for Klein, assemble a constellation of anxiety, schizoid mechanisms, and defenses against persecutory objects—such as omnipotence, splitting, and denial. How can a vicious circle lead anywhere else?

From what Klein repeatedly termed as "that vicious circle," she then proposed an opening onto a new subjective position, the depressive position (Britzman 2016). The thing is, somehow, from such mental anguish, disquieting imagination emerges from its origin in persecutory anxiety but now as tattered, worried, and rendered fragile by caring for the other and by accepting the other's care. That evening in the seminar, we were speaking of the paranoid/schizoid and depressive positions. Questions continued: Why did Klein conceptualize the emotional world through anxiety over its destruction? Why link the source of imagination to primal agonies such as those Donald Winnicott wrote of in his 1963 (1989) discussion, "Fear of Breakdown"? Winnicott, by the way, named five primal agonies: falling forever, fragmentation, depersonalization, de-realization, and isolation without any means of communication. They are primal because each experience feels as if it is an end to itself.

That evening the graduate seminar was working through a beautiful sentence of Klein, one that performed a great leap from imagining what this anguish feels like to defending against feelings. Klein had to think about what happens for the self while projecting and splitting the object relation into good and bad. Just at the point of exhaustion, at the height of sadism and its frustration, however, Klein found something new: the urge for reparation, concern for the object and the self, and a desire for a creative life.

Klein's 1935 (1975) paper "A Contribution to the Psychogenesis of Manic-Depressive States," written after the death of her son, describes that painful and panicked emotional situation:

> One of the earliest methods of defense against the dread of persecutors, whether conceived of as existing in the external world or internalized ... is the denial of psychical reality; this may result in a considerable restriction of the mechanisms of introjection and projection and in the denial of external reality. . . .(262)

> The ego then finds itself confronted with the psychical reality that its loved objects are in a state of fragmentation—in bits—and the despair, remorse and anxiety deriving from this recognition are at the bottom of numerous anxiety-situations. To quote only a few of them: there is anxiety how to put the bits together in the right way and at the right time; how to pick out the good bits and do away with the bad ones; how to bring the object to life when it has been put together; and there is the anxiety of being interfered with in this task by bad objects and one's own hatred, etc. (269)

Klein was trying to put into words how it is that we fall apart and then, ever so slowly, try to put back the pieces. She may have been asking about her own painful loss of her son. What do we have to do to tolerate emptiness, the confusion of good and bad, the sorrow of being left behind, and the frustration of not knowing yet needing to know why?

Then, too, there is a situation that causes us to defend against the search for meaning and that, when speaking of teacher education, Maxine Greene (1978) termed such absence as attractions to "the matter of mystification." I read this essay and many of her others before I met Maxine Greene and, by 1985 when I completed my doctoral studies and entered the stormy seas of higher education, I met Maxine and became what I think of as a friend. Looking back, what stands out for me was how quickly Maxine could touch on her personal preoccupations and anxieties while also feeling the challenges of thinking freely.

I am thinking about Maxine Greene's notion of imagination through wild restlessness that at times, founders in the void. Greene insisted that our best model for thinking the thought of capacious imagination and to ponder what destroys it belongs to the affecting arts. Such immersion into aesthetic conflicts is not only for the study of imagination, itself ongoing, trying, and subject to failure. The arts are also the work needed if imagination is to overcome quietism, compliance, thoughtlessness, malefic benevolence, indifference, and, as Kant would say, our haphazard melancholia. It would be, for Greene, the work of disquieting the imagination with incompleteness and allusions for the mind and heart such as what we search for and find in great visual art, theater, music, and literature. In the language of psychoanalysis, we would have to want to symbolize our aesthetic conflicts, and learn more from our search with those big ongoing questions that debate the contentions and losses of beauty, truth, meaning, and being. We would have to imagine our relationship to objects and to each other in the world as contributing something more than on offer.

The disquieting of imagination I am trying to reach, however, begins with Klein's insistence that our earliest infantile anxiety situations are needed to set the stage for the problems Maxine Greene has given us to think. Imagination is not a nice thing. In Greene's *The Dialectic of Freedom*, published in 1988, we meet so many aesthetic conflicts. Greene writes her way into the indeterminacy of freedom, an oscillation between culture and nature, self and other, and madness and sanity. Early in *Dialectic*, Greene names the thematic she develops:

> When people cannot name alternatives, imagine a better state of things, share with others a project for change, they are likely to remain anchored or submerged, even as they proudly assert their autonomy. The same is true when people uproot themselves, when they abandon families, take to the road, become strangers in desperate efforts to break loose from pre-established orders and controls. (9)

But to study the failure of imagination is to encounter a breakdown in meaning and its emotional ties and confront instead a social hatred of symbolization that does indicate a denial of psychical reality. I recall that Maxine once told me that *The Dialectic of Freedom* was a rewriting of an earlier 1973 book, *The Teacher as Stranger*. There we can trace Greene's earlier insistence: "the teacher as stranger" must be a searcher for his or her freedom, and the search involves both our primal agonies and the desire to go on.

In a letter Maxine wrote to me on October 16, 2003, when she was still at work on a typewriter, albeit with some broken keys, I received what I still think of as a 'you of all people' message. She did cushion her charge, though I admit feeling the force of her wrath. Negations aside, I was not up to fighting with Maxine. She had this talent to both kiss and slap, and this was one of those letters. Maxine was angry with one of my papers in which I discussed Phillip Roth's (2000) novel *The Human Stain*. She noticed this paper, written with my friend Don Dippo, as it was in a collection of work on critical theory, we titled "Admitting a Perhaps: Maxine Greene and Critical

Theory" (Britzman and Dippo 2003). Of course, she would read this paper in which we discussed literature and Maxine Greene. As for writing on Phillip Roth, I must admit he is not my favorite Roth: I prefer the European Joseph Roth and then also the American Henry Roth, who, in his seventies, recovered from a forty-year writing block and told us why. But it was Phillip Roth's sexism that bothered her the most. Maxine did tell me my quotations from Roth's character 'Zuckerman' were appropriate. The play *Copenhagen*, she wrote—where the truth escaped from the character's reasoning—was a much better way to discuss her topic. The topic, of course, was indeterminacy. There are more remarkable literary tributes to indeterminacy, and she mentions *Madame Bovary* with a paragraph-long sentence:

> I taught Madame Bovary for the umpteenth time the other day, rediscovered it in many ways—the way in which patriarchy infantilizes, the narrowing of choices to sexual adventures or mere misery, the complicity of the church, of the convent, the triumph of positivism at the end—after the suicide, the fate of Berthe, a remarkable nudge to self-reflection and to, "I don't know."

And yes, poor little Berthe is the child who ends the novel as an orphan and faces the terrors of the Industrial Revolution.

And that was the letter where Maxine's "I don't know," returned as a question of what to make of her existential situation: "Being old" she wrote, "refusing to be retired... I learned that one does not cry when one is alone." She ended that letter with a memory of me. Around 1987, Maxine was visiting the State University of New York at Binghamton, where, along with Wendy Kohli, I taught. At the time of her visit, Maxine had difficulty eating. She remembered I urged her to eat a baked potato. That was one of my self-cures for melancholia. Today, I understand melancholia as the self-cure.

Our letter correspondence lasted about twenty years. And there we did rehearse things that bothered us, that drove us crazy and disquieted the imagination. A card came in 2006 and Maxine's handwriting, always distinct in its strong hand, had grown weak. The willowy writing looked as if a spider had walked across the page. Stuffed in the card was a torn-off half-page. It was typewritten and with an added handwritten note telling me she had forgotten to send it. She was congratulating me on completing my psychoanalytic training and remembers those colleagues in her own time who were interested in psychoanalysis and barred from the conversations. She was reminding me of diminishing education. Again, she wrote of her isolation, not so much from colleagues but from consciousness itself. How hard it is, she tells me, to be very old. And then she wrote: "Today must be grouch day." Next time she would write me and speak of theory.

The years of her letters are still for me a life raft in the stormy seas of what often feels to me as ridiculous education. Snuck into all her listed activities—too many invitations, too much writing, too little time—were her worries about meaninglessness, not only through having to fight off the avalanche of clichés that leave us stupid. She was also worried about bereft places where there are no words. What worried her most was that consciousness recedes.

But what a time it is when consciousness roars and does so to rage against injustices. In 1989, the Corcoran Museum in Washington, D.C., refused to show the homoerotic photographs of Robert Mapplethorpe. The photographs were also banned in Cincinnati and deemed obscene. It was a particularly terrible year of government led homophobia. Maxine Greene's talk that year at the American Educational Research Association defended Mapplethorpe's art and our academic freedom to discuss love and cultural fear. Later, Maxine told me she disagreed with Mapplethorpe's homoerotic art. She said it was not her thing. What was her thing, if I could put it this way, was that she cared to demand our right to "difficult freedom," a phrase I borrow from Emanuel Levinas (1997). For Maxine, I think, it was the freedom and burden of a stranger, to enter a sort of estrangement needed to be affected by what I have called 'difficult knowledge' that, if held closely, gives birth to the insistences of the human condition as the right to pleasure and sexuality and as the right and responsibility taken to place education into a question (Britzman 1998).

Sometimes, when I am about to begin writing a new paper, I experience the pain of beginnings. I recall the demands of my undergraduate teacher in Afro-American literature, Julius Lester at the University of Massachusetts. Lester impressed upon me the importance of the first sentence. I walk to my bookshelf and play a little game. I read the first sentence of many books and marvel over their evocative power. So, I return to Maxine's books. Her first sentences take the world apart. *Teacher as Stranger* begins with the problem of education and asks what she calls "extreme questions" like: "Why transmit a heritage conceived to be sterile or "sick"? Why keep a declining culture alive?" (1973, 4). Maxine was speaking to teachers, writing against depersonalization, and asking what it means to choose to think and then open oneself to works of art. Sounding a bit like Adorno, Maxine demanded we question technological rationality in "the scientific age." She told us why we must challenge the Hegelian absolute. The sickness of education was her constant theme, and she found its unreasonable reasons and then its anxiety that results in the killing off of imagination.

Maxine, it must be said, took on the big questions from art to science, from education to philosophy, from literature to life. Her writing is an index of her reading, and her reach into the world of art, theater, and literature was wide, serious, and demanding. She expected her readers to know something, to say what is on their minds, and to be affected. I think she tried to believe that great art saves our minds, saves us from the isolation of despair, and in its examination of the unsaid and the mysteries of desire, brings solace. She always wondered why education keeps forgetting that. Maxine Greene made education bigger, more important, more searching, more indeterminable, more literary, and, yes, more emotionally and intellectually honest. And it seemed she had this big heart that, like any big heart, could be easily broken. Perhaps this is the 'otherwise' she was always writing toward and finding along the way our anxieties, discomforting truths, and wrongheaded, cruel directions. She spoke not of accountability but of responsibility. She hated the endless charts that promised completion. There is, she reminded us, the dialectics of freedom, lost and found in private life and the public sphere. Her passion was in disquieting consciousness and in the painful work of linking imagination to morality, ethics, and critique.

The last time I met Maxine was during a 2008 American Educational Research Association meeting in New York City, where our dear friend, Dr. Janet Miller, was receiving a lifetime award. By then, Maxine was into her nineties and in a wheelchair. Standing next to her was my old friend and hers, Bill Ayres. I leaned over to her and whispered, "Maxine, it's me, Deborah." She said in her raspy voice, "I know. How is your practice?" That brought me to smile, for she also wrote a preface to my first book, *Practice Makes Practice* (Britzman 2003). The word 'practice' sums it up. Maxine believed deeply that words affect us, that we have to think with them but there the trouble begins. Mainly for Maxine literature is the playground for our emotional life, for catching the unsaid in our social attitudes, for studies in incompleteness, and for confrontation between the I-know and I-don't-know. And yes, we need to be reminded that anxiety cannot be left to its own accord. We must symbolize and make the world significant. We must learn to break open something between us that is unknown to even ask, What happens for us and for others in our search for freedom?

Two associations from the psychoanalytic archive help me conclude. The first is a dream that ends Clare Winnicott's (1989) reflections on the life of D.W. Winnicott. They were happily married. She had the dream two-and-a-half years after his death:

> I dreamt that we were in our favorite shop in London, where there is a circular staircase to all floors. We were running up and down these stairs grabbing things here, there, and everywhere as Christmas presents for our friends. We were really having a spending spree.... I suddenly realized that Donald was alive after all and I thought with relief, "Now I shan't have to worry about the Christmas card." Then we were sitting in the restaurant having our morning coffee as usual. We were facing each other, elbows on the table, and I looked at him full in the face and said: "Donald there's something we have to say to each other, some truth that we have to say, what is it?" With his very blue eyes looking unflinchingly into mine he said: "That this is a dream." I replied slowly: "Oh yes, of course, you died, you died a year ago." He reiterated my words: "Yes, I died a year ago." (18)

The artist and author Adrian Stokes (2014) and friend to Melanie Klein presents the search for meaning as enigmatic. He was involved in what can be thought of as psychoanalytic art. In a paper titled "Modes of Art and Modes of Being" we are urged to look again:

> Whereas the finished work, or the work as a whole, symbolizes integration, once again while we contemplate and follow out the element of attack and its recompense, we are in touch with a process that seems to be happening on our looking, a process to which we are joined as if to an alternation of part objects. (77)

I am trying to communicate my incompleteness, the pain of reparation, my worries that consciousness recedes, and my gratitude for Maxine's Greene's life and work. And yes, in our search for the sources of affect, we also find the source of our inspirations.

Bibliography

Britzman, Deborah. 1998. *Lost Subjects, Contested Objects: Toward a Psychoanalytic Inquiry of Learning*. Albany: State University of New York Press.

———. 2003. *Practice Makes Practice: A Critical Study of Learning to Teach*. Revised edition. Albany: State University of New York Press. (Originally published in 1991).

———. 2016. *Melanie Klein: Early Analysis, Play, and the Question of Freedom*. London: Springer Press.

———, and Dippo, Don. 2003. "Admitting a Perhaps: Maxine Greene and Critical Theory." In *Critical Theory and the Human Condition: Founders and Praxis*, edited by Michael Peters, Colin Lankshear, and Mark Olssen, 130–42. New York: Peter Lang Press.

Forman, Maurice Buxton, ed. 1960. *The Letters of John Keats*. 4th ed. London: Oxford University Press.

Greene, Maxine. 1973. *The Teacher as Stranger*. New York: Wadsworth Press.

———. 1978. "The Matter of Mystification: Teacher Education in Unquiet Times." In *Landscapes of Learning*, 53–73. New York: Teachers College Press.

———. 1986. "In Search of Critical Pedagogy." *Harvard Educational Review* 56 (4): 427–41.

———. 1988. *The Dialectic of Freedom*. New York: Teachers College Press.

Klein, Melanie. (1935) 1975. A Contribution to the Psychogenesis of Manic-Depressive States. In *Love, Guilt and Reparation and Other Works, 1921–1945*, 290–305. London: Hogarth Press.

Levinas, Emmanuel. 1997. *Difficult Freedom: Essays on Judaism*. Translated by Sean Hand. Baltimore, MD: John Hopkins Press.

Roth, Philip. 2000. *The Human Stain*. New York: Vintage Books.

Stokes, Adrian. 2014. "Modes of Art and Modes of Being." In *Art and Analysis: An Adrian Stokes Reader*, edited by Meg Harris, 51–68. London: Karnac Books.

Winnicott, Clair. 1989. "D.W.W.: A Reflection." In *Psycho-Analytic Explorations*, edited by Clare Winnicott, Ray Shepherd, and Madeleine Davis, 1–18. Cambridge, MA: Harvard Educational Press.

Winnicott, Donald W. (1963) 1989. "Fear of breakdown." In *Psycho-Analytic Explorations*, edited by Clare Winnicott, Ray Shepherd, and Madeleine Davis, 87–95. Cambridge, MA: Harvard Educational Press.

About the Author

Deborah P. Britzman is Distinguished Research Professor at York University in Toronto, a Fellow of the Royal Society of Canada, and a working psychoanalyst. Known for her work in psychoanalysis and studies in the histories of difficult knowledge and critical pedagogy, Britzman is the author of nine books, of which the most recent are *A Psychoanalyst in the Classroom; Freud and Education; Melanie Klein: Early Analysis, Play, and the Question of Freedom.*

Index

A
acceptance, 6, 9–10, 67, 91, 113
Adorno, Theodor, 23, 50
aesthetic conflicts, 114–115
affect, 45, 70, 108
    Also see anxiety
aggression, 15, 33, 37, 72
AIDS, vii-xviii, 13, 29
    and education 33–34, 37
ambivalence, 30, 34, 46, 106
anticipation, xi, xvi, 6
anxiety, xi, 6–7, 10, 17, 30, 36–37, 80–81, 108–110, 113
Arendt, Hannah, 23–24, 26, 49, 50, 64–65
audacity, 77

B
Babel, Isaac, 51–52
Balint, Alice, 32
Barthes, Roland, 14
belief, xiii, xvii, 11, 91, 97
Bion, Wilfred, 47, 64–65, 76–77
Bollas, Christopher, 31, 39n5

C
Cameron, Laura, 101
Canguilhem, Georges, 39n1, 67
care, xii, 14, 16, 70
Caruth, Cathy, 23
Castoriadis, Cornelius, 66
Certeau, Michael de, 45
childhood, 1–2, 15, 90, 96, 98
clinical supervision, 76–77
confusion, xi, 26, 111, 114
    as defence, 43–46
countertransference, xv
creativity, 5– 8, 11–12, 75, 82, 109
cure, 67
currere, 14–15
curriculum, 41–46

D
death, 45–47
defense mechanisms, 17, 32–34, 95, 113
    Also see ego
Delany, Samuel, 34–36, 40n8
Deleuze, Gilles, xiv
denial, 7, 13, 55, 61,108–109, 114
    and denial of denial, 33, 39n5
    and socio–political forms of, 55, 61–63, 65, 104
depression, 7, 18, 53, 56, 64, 67, 96, 101, 110

depressive position, 17, 110, 111, 113–114
    and paranoid–schizoid position, 17, 113–114
    Also see Melanie Klein
desire, 78–79, 84–87, 90–91
difference, 7–9, 110, 108–109
difficult knowledge, xvii, 22–24, 62, 117
dreams, xv, xvi, 32, 59, 65, 72, 90, 93, 97, 101, 118
drives, xv, 16–17, 102

E
education, xi, xii, 6, 104
    and crisis, 20–24, 61–62
    and human conduct, 102, 103
    as interference, 91–92
    as predicament, 15, 102–103
    as state of mind, xviii, 50, 59–61, 73
ego, 17, 29–34, 36–37, 39n3, 83, 114
    Also see anxiety and defense mechanisms
Ehrenberg, Alain, 66–67
emotional situations, xi, xvi, 15, 67, 69, 91–92, 107–108
    Also see Melanie Klein
empathy, 6, 111
    and identificatory engagement, 109–110
Erickson, Erik, 39n3
experience, xi–xii, 2, 21, 22, 60, 61, 67, 80–81

F
Felman, Shoshana, 16, 22
Ferenczi, Sándor, 52–53
Fliess, Wilhelm, 91
Forrester, John, xiv, xvi, 101–103, 108
Foucault, Michael, 14
fragmentation, 17–18
frame, 6
free association, 91
freedom, xvii, xix, 22, 31, 117
Freire, Paulo, 1
Freud, Anna, 25–26, 91–92, 104
Freud, Sigmund, 2, 17, 52–53, 65, 79, 101–102
    on constructions and working through, 90–91
    on egoism, 29–32
    on resistance, 32–33, 94–95
    and touch, 33
    on war, mourning, and melancholia, 41–47
frustration, 17, 61, 65, 79, 81, 114

G
Gardner, Robert, 24
gay and lesbian literature, 12–15, 34–36, 40n8
Green, André, 61, 63
Greene, Maxine, 113–118

H
homoerotic histories, 14, 17–18
Haver, William, 32, 34, 45
helplessness, 69
 Also see frustration

I
idealization, 8
identificatory thought, 32
illness, 30
 and health, 39n2, 70
imagination, 6–8, 113–115
incompleteness, xvi, xviii, 110
infancy, 8–9, 107–108
influence, xviii
inhibition, xiv, xvii, 5–7, 9, 18, 38, 78, 90, 99, 104
irony, 89–90
insanity, 66–67
interest, 105
internalization, 8–9
interpretation, 94–95
isolation, 23, 33
Issacs, Susan 7, 103–104

J
James, William, 24–26

K
Kierkegaard, Søren, 89
Klein, Melanie, 16–17, 30, 51, 67
 and defense of confusion, 43, 47
 and depressive position, 113
 and emotional situations, 107–109
 on phantasies, xvi–xviii, 109–111
Kristeva, Julia, xiv, 14, 49–50, 66, 70, 73, 91
Kushner, Tony, 34

L
Lacan, Jacques, 77–78
 and Ecole Freudienne de Paris 82–85
Laplanche, Jean, xvi
Lear, Jonathan, xvi, 89
learning, xvii, 32
 and destruction, 26, 91
Leavitt, David, 13
libidinal history, 32
listening, 95
love, 8, 17–18, 90–91, 101
 and hate, 91, 104, 114
 and loss, 41, 44–45, 87
Loewald, Hans, xvi
Lyotard, Jean-François, 39n6, 44–45

M
madness, 50–51, 67
 and sanity, 8, 49
Malting House Garden School, 103–104

McDougall, Joyce, 70
 and analysis with Sammy the scribe, 71–73
melancholia
 and mania, 43
 and mourning, 44–45, 50
memory, 2
 and forgetting, 17, 55
mental health, 63–64
Milner, Marion, 6–10
Musil, Robert, 42

N
narrative revolts, 12, 14, 50
 and freedom, xii, 16, 61–62, 90
 and guilt, 94
negative capability, 113

O
object relations, xvi, 6–7, 17, 69, 108
objectivity, 6, 9, 101
 and subjectivity, 7–8, 14
 and madness, 67
Oedipal complex, 91
orality, 8
 and anality, 8, 72, 104

P
pain of incompleteness, 67
Patton, Cindy, 39n4
pedagogy, 78, 102–104
phantasy, xvi, xvii, 6, 14, 16–17, 51, 90, 113
Phillips, Adam, 25
Pinar, William, 13, 16
play, 31, 16, 72, 107–108, 117
poetics, 79
primacy of the other, xv
projective identification, 17, 109
prosopographical method, 102
psychical reality, xv, 8, 43, 108
 and creativity, 9–10
psychoanalysis, xiv–xv
 and definitions of, xvi, 49–50, 73–74
 and supervision, 76–77
 and writing, 101–103

Q
queer pedagogy, 16
queer theory, 16

R
Rancière, Jacques, 69, 71
reading, 2–3, 15, 103
 and queer practices, 16
 and writing, 108
Readings, Bill, 39n7, 45
reparation, 30, 37
repression, 33

INDEX

resistance, 17, 32, 39n6, 90–91, 98
    and resistance to resistance, 95
Rose, Jacqueline, 29, 39n1, 46, 78
Roth, Joseph, 51–52
Roudinesco, Elizabeth, 83
Ruth the scribbler, 10–11

S

Sachs, Hanns, 39n3
Schuman, Sarah, 30–31
screen memories, 2
Sebald, W.G., 53–55
Sedgwick, Eve Kosofsky, 14–16
Segal, Hanna, 109
self-knowledge, 26
sexuality, 14–15
Silin, Jonathan, 31
Sliwinski, Sharon, 65
splitting, 16
Stokes, Adrian, 11–12, 118–119
superego anxiety, 36, 81, 91–92
supervision, 77–79
symbolization, 8, 16–17
symptom formation, 17, 31, 91

T

teacher education
    and conflicts in, 21–22, 26
    and supervision, 74–76, 80–82
    and trauma, 24, 26
    and manic defenses, 24–25
thinking, 9–10, 32, 39n6, 45–46, 64–65, 79, 108, 115
transference, 2, 14, 69–70, 95, 108–109
touching, 33–34

U

uncertainty, xv, 6, 10, 70
unconscious, 39n3
understanding, 103, 109–111
undoing, 33, 76
uneven development, xi, 69

V

Vattimo, Gianni, 79
verstehen, 103
vulnerability, 18, 70

W

waiting, xi, xv, xvi, 64, 69, 75
war, 23, 39n1, 43, 45–47, 53–56, 109
White, Edmund, 15
Willinsky, John, 45
Wills, Clair, 62–63
Winnicott, Clair, 118
Winnicott, D. W., 26, 31, 67, 113–114
    cases of Sarah and teacher, 95–98
working through, 17, 91, 98–99
    and mourning, 41
writing, 6–7, 10–11
    and inhibition, xvii

Y

Young-Bruehl, Elizabeth, 109–111